"Don't walk in front of me;
I may not follow.
Don't walk behind me;
I may not lead.
Walk beside me; just be
my friend"

Albert Camus

The
Friendship
Book

A THOUGHT
FOR EACH DAY | **2022**

January

THE fact that we have a whole new year ahead of us could feel daunting to some. The world might seem more chaotic than it has been before, with so many things in need of change or repair.

E.B. White, the author of "Stuart Little" and "Charlotte's Web", once received a letter from a fan who despaired about . . .

Well, just about everything.

Agreeing with his correspondent that mankind had, indeed, made a mess of things, he said he still trusted in our ability to come good in the end.

In the meantime, he added, it was up to each of us to remain steadfast in the little things. To that end, he intended to wind his seven-day clock up in the morning, so it might tick, truly and evenly, through the week ahead.

The big things of this world are generally composed of many little things, and if enough of us tick away steadily, true to the principles of love, honesty and kindness, this year will turn out as well as any there has ever been.

It might even be better than any of the others that have gone before.

SUSAN introduced him to me.

"This is Robert," she said. "He goes around quietly doing things for people, and he never gets the credit."

He looked like he was surprised she had noticed.

"Oh, it's always offered," he said. "I just don't take it. If I can give from what I've been given, that's not to my credit. That's to the credit of the One who gave me everything I have."

It's to our credit when we understand this.

THIS year is very special;
  We wonder what it holds,
With new surprises on the way
As every month unfolds.

The number is a special one
And never seen before;
It opens up the future
And all that lies in store.

Go forward with a happy heart –
Step out along the year,
And make the most of every day:
This special time is here!

Iris Hesselden

THE decorations might still be up, but I am pretty sure the remains of crackers pulled around the family dinner table will be firmly in the bin by now.

Christmas crackers are an unusual tradition, hardly known in the United States, but a staple part of the British celebration.

There is a memorial to their inventor, Thomas Smith, in Finsbury Square.

In 1847, this young confectioner travelled to Paris, where he saw bonbons: sugared almonds wrapped in a twist of paper. That twist of paper gave the basic shape of the cracker.

Thomas's unique addition was to add a love motto inside the wrapping. These would eventually become the Christmas cracker jokes!

Now, I am not going to defend those jokes, but I like the idea of a love motto.

The bonbons themselves were already sweet and a commercial success, but Thomas's idea proved there is nothing that cannot be made sweeter by simply adding a little love!

As ideas go, that's a cracker!

Shutterstock

The New Year is full of promise. Make the most of every day!

CREE is a character in J.M. Barrie's "Auld Licht Idylls". He's a poor man, a hard worker, and his mother's only support.

When he leaves town for a while, his mother takes her scribbled attempts at a letter to the school teacher for him to tidy up.

The teacher is surprised by how many endearing terms are in it, because he has never heard such words ever exchanged between them.

It turns out Cree has been teaching her to write and made up a sheet of phrases for her to practise with.

There are everyday words and statements like "the peats is near done", but there are a disproportionate number of phrases like "God watch over my Cree", "Oh, my beloved son", "Dear son Cree" and "Loving mother".

In teaching her to write, he was also – perhaps without realising it – teaching her how he wished he had been loved.

Our actions might be the best way of displaying our feelings, but there's a place in our soul that longs to hear these things.

Don't let your words of affection go unsaid.

TODAY is known as *Nollaig na mBan*, or Women's Christmas, in Ireland.

Despite moves towards equality, most of the work in any Christmas season will still be done by the women of the house.

On the sixth of January, when the decorations are finally taken down, the women try to take a little well-deserved time for themselves.

It can sometimes be a poor sort of affair, with all the good food and drink already having been consumed. But sometimes a cup of tea, a biscuit and a chat with a friend can be a real treat.

And those of us who didn't do any of the work – who simply enjoyed the end results – could do worse, once the festivities are over, than show our appreciation to those without whom the festive time would have been a lot less wonderful.

Ladies, thank you!

DO you have one of those smart speaker things? Harry's son bought him one for Christmas.

Then Harry – for some unfathomable reason – invited me in to help him to set it up.

When he eventually thought we were done, he asked it a question, but there was a problem with the internet connection at that moment, and the answer wasn't immediately available.

The device responded by saying, "I'm sorry. I am having trouble understanding right now. Please try again later."

We did try later. And we got the right answer. But that reply made me feel sympathy for the little device.

There have been many times I have had trouble understanding and wished that, instead of despairing of me, people would show me the grace of trying again later when I might be able to do better.

That reminded me that I might show others the same grace, when who knows what difficulties prevent them from giving their best response.

THE shop was bursting at the seams with shoppers looking for their January sale bargains.

There had been calls for all staff to report to the checkouts, and those who were already there were really earning their pay.

Then a man in the shop's uniform was spotted heading for the exit.

A colleague looked up from her till and yelled after him.

"You'd better not be leaving us to deal with this!" she shouted, sounding properly annoyed.

"Sorry," he replied, sounding like he meant it. "It's my daughter's birthday today and I told her I would be there for the party."

"Oh!" Her tone completely changed. "Have a great time! Tell her happy birthday from us!"

Doesn't it make such a difference when we understand why the other person does what they do?

THERE'S a Sunday school song that talks about loving God with all our heart, all our mind, all our strength and all our soul.

When they sing it, the children make a heart sign with their hands at the appropriate word.

They point to their temples at the word "mind"; they flex their muscles at the word "strength"; they tap the bottoms of their shoes when they sing "with all my soul".

For a fleeting second, I thought it a shame that this action had to be a play on the word "sole".

Then I realised that your soul should be a firm foundation – something you can safely stand on.

Monday — January 10

LISTENING to the radio, I heard artist Arabella Dorman say, "Compassion is really difficult, because it asks you to go to where people are damaged . . . where they are broken."

The next day, I talked to my friend, Susan, who had organised a free Christmas dinner for local people in need. The ones who came – and were well fed – all had problems. A very small percentage brought those problems with them.

The dinner was a success, but Susan was frazzled!

Truly compassionate people will go to those difficult places, be shaken by the experience, and go back again.

Real compassion isn't pretty, but the people who practise it are pretty amazing!

Tuesday — January 11

IHEARD of a woman who made a vow that she would never say or do anything she wouldn't be proud to have as her last words or her last act.

What do you think? A simple enough thing. Yet, undoubtedly, a difficult thing! A wise thing, perhaps, given that none can predict or control their future.

But what a difference it might make to the average life!

Keep God firmly in your heart and soul.

Shutterstock.

Wednesday — January 12

IN this part of the country, winter hasn't really kicked in yet. But autumn has come and gone and "real" winter is surely just around the corner.

Despite that, I have noticed buried bulbs pushing their leaves above the dirt.

My friend, Catherine, recently presented me with a ribbon-wrapped bunch of tulips from her garden.

Some might see this as a sign that the seasons are confused. Me? I see it as proof that the urge towards life and beauty is always with us.

Thursday — January 13

TWO hundred miles north of John O' Groats lies the island of Foula.

Because their celebrations are based on the Julian calendar rather than the Gregorian calendar like the rest of the UK, today is their New Year.

Foula folk enjoy New Year as much as anyone else. The date isn't important. The heart of the celebration is what matters.

Which goes to show that any day can be a new beginning!

Friday — January 14

THE young man on the subway bench was having difficulty with his tie. The older woman next to him noticed.

"I have an interview," he explained. "Never worn one of these before."

"My husband wore one of these every day of his working life," she replied, getting up and tying his tie for him.

I don't know if he got the job. I hope he did. What I do know is that they had lived very different lives and moved in very different circles. When their worlds had a chance to overlap, they did so in love and hope.

When people with different experiences of the world meet, may it always be like this!

Saturday — January 15

THERE is a building in Bratislava that is rumoured to be around four hundred years old.

In places, it really looks it! The plaster has come off large parts of the outside walls, and the exposed "brickwork" might more properly be called "boulderwork".

But a talented street artist has made his way around the wooden shutters covering the windows and painted beautiful Van Gogh-style pictures on them.

Where had I seen such beauty before? In the eyes of some older folk I have known. The ones who have loved their lives.

Sunday — January 16

FOR a joke, two students placed a pineapple on a table in an art exhibition. When they returned later, not only was it still there, but someone had placed a glass case over it, thinking it a genuine exhibit!

It provoked an enthusiastic discussion on the nature of art, along with many laughs. But isn't a pineapple a work of art? Isn't every aspect of nature?

We don't need to place every tree, fruit and flower under glass, but we ought to appreciate them as the works of a master artist.

Monday — January 17

IT seems there is a phone app for everything. Some of them are useful, and some less so. Recently I heard of a very useful one.

This app enables visually impaired people to point their phone at something, and a volunteer – from any part of the world – will tell them what they see.

A friend who thought they might like to help signed up. It seems there were (at the time) two hundred thousand people using the app. But there were two million volunteers waiting to be called.

The numbers will inevitably change, but it is my hope that the proportion of people willing to help to those needing help will stay the same. Or rise!

Tuesday — January 18

IF I remember it properly from my distant childhood, Winnie-the-Pooh respected Owl because that grand old bird could spell Tuesday!

Of course, Owl couldn't actually spell Tuesday properly, but Pooh understood that there were days when spelling Tuesday properly wasn't the most important thing.

We all have our strengths and weaknesses.

On some days our strengths won't be of much use. On other days our weaknesses might be the very thing the world needs.

It's a wise bear who appreciates the difference!

Wednesday — January 19

I **COMPLIMENTED** our dear friend Mary on her new coat. She told me she got it in the sales.

Then, of course, I went too far.

"But isn't it just too nice to be wearing to the shops? Shouldn't you save something that lovely for a special occasion?"

She gave me the look you might give a child you were fond of and who didn't know any better.

"This life, Francis," she told me. "This is the special occasion!"

Thursday — January 20

IN his poem "How To Be A Poet (To Remind Myself)", American writer and environmental campaigner Wendell Berry said, "There are no un-sacred places; there are only sacred places and desecrated places".

If I might be so presumptuous, I feel something the same about people.

There are those who have grown in love and those who haven't had the chance to.

Each comes from the same beginning, bearing a similar set of possibilities. Only some get to fulfil them.

But just as we might restore a desecrated place with love and effort, sometimes we can restore a life the same way.

COBWEBS of lace and ice and frost
Are threaded through the trees:
A patchwork quilt of evergreens,
A frozen glaze of leaves,
Bare branches poke like crochet hooks
That weave with every gust;
The brittle earth, all cracked with cold,
A shivering white crust.
Brave winter flowers are spread across
This frigid tapestry;
The winter seamstress shows her work
Through all this majesty.

Lily Christie

Saturday — January 22

THERE'S a time for righting wrongs. There are times to fight battles.

The poet Hafiz, from 14th-century Shiraz, suggested we take an occasional day to "talk about that which disturbs no-one".

Why? Because it would "bring some peace into those beautiful eyes". A day when we didn't complain, didn't criticise, didn't try to put things "right", but appreciated them as they are.

It might not make a difference to anyone else, but it would surely bring some peace to our soul.

Sunday — January 23

IN Christopher Fry's 1948 play "The Lady's Not For Burning", a war-weary soldier asks a judge to take his life instead of that of a condemned woman with much to live for.

"Shall we laugh?" he asks the woman.

"For what reason?" she enquires.

"For the reason of laughter, since laughter is the surest touch of genius in creation."

The things about us that aren't simply about survival, like altruism and laughter, are the surest signs we were meant for more.

Monday — January 24

IT was a lovely little poem, spontaneously sent. It had some complimentary words for a friend of mine.

What the poet didn't know was that he was having a difficult day, and those kind words unpicked all his defences and the tears started to flow.

When she heard what she'd done, she felt awful. But he insisted she shouldn't.

"Tears heal," he said. "I am sure I'll be better after a good cry".

And he was.

This, surely, is why we put kindness out there into the world, not knowing for certain what good it will do, but trusting it will find its own wonderful purpose.

Tuesday — January 25

LILLIAN GISH starred in one of the most successful films of Hollywood's "silent era", "The Birth Of A Nation".

Her film career spanned seven decades, and she was also a writer and director. She died just short of her hundredth birthday.

Speaking of ageing while still in her sixties, she said, "I ignore every effect of age. Except for wisdom. That I accept."

I believe we are here to learn and to love. Age, approached properly, teaches us to do each of those better.

Wednesday — January 26

AT the grand old age of thirty-eight, June decided she wanted to be a writer. A year later, she showed me a message from a publisher. They wanted to publish her novel!

Something we said caught the attention of her five-year-old daughter. She tugged her mum's sleeve and asked, "When will I be too old to chase my dream?"

June patted her daughter's hand and said, "Never!"

I can't wait to see her last year's work in print. But even more than that, I hope I get to see the results of that one word, spoken to an attentive little girl.

TAKE pleasure in each moment
As the world begins to stir.
The birdsong in the tree tops,
A cat's welcoming purr,
Shafts of golden sunlight,
Streaming through the pane,
The smell of fresh-made coffee,
All remind you once again
That life keeps on renewing,
However you may feel.
Each morning is a precious gift
And this new day is real.
Embrace the hours before you;
Create yourself a plan,
And give your day a purpose –
Make of it what you can!

Marian Cleworth

I WAS grumpy. When Mary asked why, I told her about a man who, for no obvious reason, had been rude to someone.

She thought a moment, then asked me, "What's sixty times sixty?"

I amazed myself by answering, "Three thousand, six hundred."

I balked when she asked me to multiply that by 24, so she gave me a pen and paper to work it out.

"Eighty-six thousand, four hundred."

"Those are the seconds you have in your day," she told me. "How many did he steal from you while being unpleasant?"

I guessed about 180.

"And how many more of your precious seconds have you voluntarily donated to his unpleasantness?"

I actually started to count. She saw that and laughed.

"The correct answer is too many!"

People or situations will cast a shadow over our time. If we can't help them shine brighter, then we should make sure those tarnished seconds don't spoil the golden ones we have left.

Saturday — January 29

FRIENDS from the United States told me about a recent Amish barn-moving.

The farmer who owned the barn – which was 150 feet long – wanted it moved from one field to another and turned to face in a different direction.

Two hundred and fifty men gathered. They picked the barn up and carried it to its new location!

The Amish eschew modern technology, and many of us would think this a sacrifice. On the other hand, if they can call on 250 friends to pick up a barn for them, perhaps they haven't sacrificed the truly important things.

Sunday — January 30

WELL done on being a helping hand," he said to the woman behind the counter.

"No, no," she replied, downplaying whatever had happened. "It was just a case of being in the right place at the right time."

"Aye, aye," he said as he walked towards the door. "Good hearts tend to find themselves there a lot."

I finished my tea, wondering. Do they find themselves there so often because they pay more attention to other people? Or are they drawn there by a higher power who knows the bigger picture, who values good hearts and knows how to use them as the answers to other people's prayers?

Who can tell? Possibly the best way to know is to keep on being a "good heart" until we figure it out.

Monday — January 31

THE book was falling to bits. It had been presented as a school prize in 1871. Written by W.H.G. Kingston some time before that, the tatty volume bore the embossed title "Ralph Clavering". Inside was the subtitle, "We Must Try Before We Can Do".

Thinking of the people that thought must have inspired over the years of its existence, I found it a safe place on my bookshelf, patted it gently and said, "Thanks for trying. You've done well".

A sense of community is a worthy pursuit.

Pennsylvania, USA.

Shutterstock.

February

Tuesday — February 1

IT might not feel like spring has sprung, but today, in Celtic traditions, is Imbolc, the beginning of spring.

It's a time of confident expectancy, a time when things are in bud and will surely flower. There's a feeling of having survived the worst of winter and anything from here on in must surely be better.

With weather patterns the way they are these days, that might not always be the case. Perhaps the seasons were more firmly fixed in their routine back when the tradition began.

Of course, apart from the occasional storm, things do as a whole start to get better. From this day on, we move further away from the winter solstice and ever closer to the spring equinox.

So hold fast! We are getting there. Things will be better!

Wednesday — February 2

CANDLEMAS is a traditional day of thanks for the candles that shone their light in churches, seeing them through winter, in the days before gas and electricity did the job.

In my own younger days, I often went upstairs to bed carefully holding a candle and marvelling at the shadows on the walls. In my memories of those days is a great feeling of comfort. Why?

Well, where did the light come from? From the flame? But it was not the same as the light. From wax around a cotton wick? But they were not the light. From the chemicals on the end of the matchstick? But they were not the light. From the scrape of flint against metal? But they were not the light.

How could light come from all these things that were not light? Perhaps it was already in them, waiting for some process or event to set it free. Perhaps the light is in everything.

Perhaps the light is in you and me. Just waiting to be set free.

Shine your light!

Thursday — February 3

RUTH COLLIE was an English-born Canadian poet. In a lovely little fancy, she had Life, disguised as a pedlar, stop by her window. She said she might buy some of his wares and asked what he had to offer.

He opened his pack and showed her soft clouds with crimson folds, birds with shining wings, laughter, a moonbeam, music, love and light.

"How much?" she asked.

"Pay me naught," the pedlar replied. "Take your share."

Friday — February 4

*W*HEN *spirits tend to get quite low,*
  With winter weather on the go,
Take a walk and look around –
Green shoots are bursting through the ground.
Snowdrops growing in bright array
Bring some brightness to the day.
Simple things that do amaze
In the midst of cold, drab days,
Surprises that you're bound to find,
Are sure to lift your frame of mind.
Ever full is nature's book,
If we only care to look.

Pamela Ramage

Saturday — February 5

STANDING in the Chinese takeaway, Harry realised he had exactly the right coins in his hand to pay for his meal. He counted them out and took a seat.

A moment later, a boy of about ten years old came over and handed him five pence, saying he'd dropped it.

Harry saw the boy's friends giggling and making fun of him. He put the coin in his pocket. His hand came out with a pound coin.

"Have this for your honesty," he told the surprised boy.

"If we want to have kind adults in the world," Harry told me later, "we have to show kind children that it's worth the risk."

Sunday — February 6

ROBERT LOUIS STEVENSON "built" some great works of literature. His father, Thomas Stevenson, was an engineer who built some great lighthouses.

RLS dedicated one of his books to his father: "by whose devices the great sea lights in every quarter of the world now shine more brightly."

The rest of us might never be literary giants or physically illuminate dangerous seas, but if, in faith and love, we can light up a corner of the world for our brother or sister, then we, too, will have helped build a better world.

Monday — February 7

MARGARET-JANE insisted she was going to give up. She'd tried to help someone and they'd taken advantage of her kindness.

Perhaps, she thought, she shouldn't even bother trying any more.

An old farming saying came to mind.

Back when seeds were scattered over fields by hand, the sower might calculate their return with the "equation": "One for the mouse, one for the crow, one to rot and one to grow."

I shared it with her and started to explain my thinking. But she got there first!

"Are you trying to tell me," she asked, "that if we want our kindness to take root, we might need to sacrifice a few attempts at goodness for the sake of the one that would grow?"

"I was!" I confirmed.

She smiled and said, "Then I will!"

Tuesday — February 8

WHEN I hesitate to help someone because I disapprove of the way the person lives their life, I remind myself that I don't know what pains might have driven them to those self-destructive choices.

I also try to remember the German proverb: "Charity sees the need, not the cause".

Portland Bill Lighthouse, Dorset.

Shutterstock.

Be a light in the life of
the people you love.

Wednesday — February 9

DESCRIBING Andy Warhol as a conceptual artist as well as a pop artist, a radio commentator told his listeners that Warhol "once vacuumed an entire gallery as a work of art".

I almost laughed out loud. Then I remembered the people of faith who, for centuries, have performed the most menial of jobs as devotions to God.

Perhaps we laugh too easily. Perhaps, if we look closely enough at anything done for the love of it, we will find art and God.

Thursday — February 10

HARRY had finally got around to pruning his rose bushes. The snipping was the easy bit, but I winced as he went to pick up the thorny cuttings without his gardening gloves on.

"Ow!" I cried in sympathy. "Those must jag!"

Carrying on regardless, Harry turned to me.

"How hard they are to pick up depends on how hard I pick them up."

A gentle hand helps make most situations less prickly is what I think my wise friend was saying.

Friday — February 11

THE Lady Of The House and I were out, pushing a pram with a five-week-old baby sleeping in it.

When we returned the little one to his mother, she asked why there was money in his pram. We told her it was a tradition. She had never heard of it.

In times gone by, and perhaps only in certain areas, the tradition when you first met a newborn was to drop some silver in its pram. It might have been a sixpence, if it could be spared.

The cash that accumulated there might be a very real help to the parents, but it was more than that. It was a sort of commitment to the baby's wellbeing, saying that we – individually and together – will help raise you.

Far too loving a tradition to let fade away.

I **HEARD** a story about hot water softening spaghetti, hardening an egg and making a refreshing drink out of tea leaves.

The point was that the difficult situation isn't as important as what we make of it.

The notion dates back to Francis Bacon in the early 17th century – and earlier! For he quoted some unnamed source in "The Historie Of Life And Death" when he wrote, "The same fire hardens clay and causes wax to melt away".

The effect our trouble will have, it seems, depends not on the troubles, but on what we are going into them.

Sunday — February 13

IF I said that one sentence in the Bible covered three whole verses, people might reasonably expect it to be quite lengthy. It's not.

Whoever divided the Bible into verses took the line "Rejoice always, pray continually, give thanks in all circumstances, for this is God's will for you in Christ Jesus" and broke it into three parts.

Perhaps they wanted us to take the "bullet points" in 1 Thessalonians 5:16-18 more seriously: "Rejoice always"; "Pray continually"; "Give thanks, always".

What a difference that one sentence could make!

Monday — February 14

L OVE knows no distinction
And with time it doesn't wait,
But sometimes it can coincide
With a certain, special date.
And when it does you may feel that
You must communicate
This moment when love has conspired
Your heart to captivate
With a card where words can best decribe
Your altered, happy state.

John Darley

How many conflicts could be solved if we met face to face?

Shutterstock.

Tuesday — February 15

IF ever you are wandering through Darvel in East Ayrshire, you might come across a memorial wall to local man and successful industrialist Alexander Morton.

On his memorial plaque are these words by English naturalist and writer Denys Watkins-Pitchford.

"The wonder of the world, the beauty and the power, the shape of things, their colours, lights and shades, these I saw. Look ye also while life lasts."

I am guessing that Alexander Morton did. The question now is: will we also? Even in February there is much that is wonderful to look at – if we will!

Wednesday — February 16

TWO of our neighbours have dogs. If someone walks along the path between their houses, one might bark. The other will bark in response. Hearing that bark, the first will bark louder. Pretty soon they are both barking frantically and can hardly be told apart.

Recently, the two neighbours got together and the dogs played together like puppies! The next day they went back to barking at each other across the path.

Human beings aren't so very different. When we are separated, physically, socially or via electronic gadgetry, we tend to suspect the worse and respond defensively. But when we meet up, we generally find less to react against and more to like.

Whenever we can, let's decrease the distances between us.

Thursday — February 17

IT must have been their version of saying Grace. The meals had arrived, but the family at the table next to ours didn't immediately pick up their cutlery.

The mother began with, "Today, I am grateful for . . ." Then the children took turns listing the things they appreciated. The last one, a girl of about ten, said, "And what are you thankful for, Dad?"

He took a deep breath and, with heartfelt sincerity, said, "Two things. Right here. And right now."

PSST! Over here!" Her tone sounded so urgent that I only thought about protesting before hunkering down in the long grass.

How could I not be intrigued? Eight-year-old Esme was focused on the window of her garden hut and the birds flitting around it.

The previous year I had advised her mum about a wasps' nest in there. Nature had run its course: the wasps had left, never to return. Esme had been fascinated to hear that they gathered material for their nests by biting bits of fences, decking, whatever wood they could find, and mulching it up.

Her garden fence was stained green and there were plenty of green streaks in the structure.

"Recycling," Esme whispered.

I admitted to being confused.

"The birds are taking bits of the wasps' nest," she explained. "They're using it to make their own nests in those trees over there.

"They'll lay eggs in the nest and after the chicks hatch and learn to fly, the nests will fall off the tree and fertilise the ground for more trees to grow. And maybe we'll make green fences out of them!"

She stopped to catch her breath and see if I understood.

I understood two things. There is no teacher (or recycler) like Mother Nature. And no student as keen to learn as an eight-year-old child!

THE Nursing Association published the picture as part of a programme to support trainees who had family commitments. It showed a group of young trainee nurses. One held a baby-sized mannequin of the kind used to teach resuscitation.

But she held it in the crook of her arm and looked lovingly at it, like she might a real baby. Perhaps because of this the woman beside her seemed to have instinctively reached over and stroked the baby's cheek with a fingertip.

Perhaps it was just carefully staged, but it made me think. How we treat people sets a standard for others.

Make that standard a good one. Make it a loving one.

Sunday — February 20

MARGARET BARBER usually wrote about the Devonshire countryside, but visiting London once, she stopped at a wharf on the Thames to watch exotic cargoes being unloaded.

"The river speaks of citizenship in the great world of God," she wrote, "wherein all men have place, each man has his own place, and everyone should be neighbour to him who might have need."

Monday — February 21

DRIVING is a new experience for Emily.

"A couple of times I have been casual with my indicating," she told me. "I would indicate and move almost at the same time. Sometimes I got away with it. Sometimes it has led to some horn-tooting.

"But if I indicate, then wait a few seconds so everyone understands what I am about to do, things go much more smoothly.

"It made me wonder. What if I wasn't so quick to react in other aspects of my life? What if I took a few seconds to make sure I fully understood what was happening?"

It all indicated to me that Emily is on the road to a wiser, smoother and more peaceful life.

Tuesday — February 22

THE two dogs had been allowed off the lead so they could run off some excess energy. And, of course, to make their day complete they had found a muddy puddle to run through.

The golden retriever, when it returned, was only golden from the knees up. But the Jack Russell was muddy up to its chin. From the same puddle!

I couldn't help but smile, and then think. Sometimes I might be tempted to wonder why people make such a fuss about their difficulties.

The dogs reminded me that, while some problems might seem a walk in the park to me, for others . . . Well, they might be up to their necks in it.

THERE'S an old Scots proverb I am very fond of. It goes, "Mony a mickle maks a muckle".

The spelling varies, but basically it translates as "lots of little things make a big thing".

A man might make a decent income by being good at many little jobs; lots of people doing a little bit to help someone adds up to that someone being helped in a big way.

But I think the Russian version of that old saying expresses it best.

"If everyone gave a thread, the poor man would have a shirt."

Thursday — February 24

TOM is a hillwalker.

"That last step you take before you reach the summit," he told me, "is the most tired you will be on that journey. The next step brings the often breathtaking view from the summit, the panoramic vista – and your tiredness gets forgotten.

"It's the same in life. The time when you are most tired is when you are closest to giving up. But it's also when you are closest to wonders you might never have imagined."

Friday — February 25

WHO doesn't love a compliment?
They cheer us, and elate;
They make us proud of what we've done –
Receiving them is great!
So let us not forget, in turn,
To give them out as well,
For words may make more difference than
We ever can foretell.
So if you feel some praise is due,
Don't feel too shy to say.
The very least your words will do
Is brighten someone's day!

Maggie Ingall

The last step before the summit is the hardest – but don't give up!

The Lake District.

Shutterstock.

Saturday — February 26

WE live in a world of wonders. Much that is taken for granted today was science-fiction in my youth.

Things I do without thinking in my old age could never have been done at the time of my birth. I cannot begin to comprehend the sort of world today's babies will grow up into – although I trust and believe they will do amazing things with it.

Charles Alexandre de Calonne was an ingenious man, and may have saved the court of Louis XVI from going bankrupt, but I doubt if even he could have imagined how his words would have seemed today, when he said: "Madam, if a thing is possible, consider it done. If it is impossible, it shall be done"!

Sunday — February 27

WHEN the minister asked people to craft a poem from their experiences of God, he didn't expect much.

Only two of the congregation tried it.

Their poems appeared in the next newsletter and somehow a copy made its way on to the pavement, where a passer-by picked it up.

The next issue had a letter from a man who had given up on God long ago, but the love in the poems reminded him of how much he missed that relationship.

The following week, he was in church.

Monday — February 28

IN his 1949 book "Delight", J.B. Priestley wrote about the different attitudes towards dress that men and women had. Men were charitable in their self-image and thus usually dressed badly. But women discussing clothes in a group were altogether more realistic: "Kate's left shoulder is higher than her right; Meg is very broad across the hips; Phyllis has very short legs."

These comments, he thought, were never made to hurt. They were accepted fact, and the main purpose of the gathering was to come up with ways to make the facts more beautiful!

If only we could work that way in, say, politics, spending less time arguing and putting more effort into making things better!

34

March

IT was a rare day. Windy, but with no sign of cloud in the sky. George had taken the chance to hang a washed dog blanket out to dry.

As we made to leave the garden for our walk, he turned to look at that patch of flapping green material.

"Doesn't everything look better against a clear blue sky?" he asked.

And he was right. As part of a larger wash it would never have been noticed and nothing would have been thought of it. But being framed in beauty seemed to ask more of the old blanket and, in this instance, it had responded. It really was a lovely shade of green.

Frame yourself, surround yourself, not with people who make you look better, but with people (or a faith) who by their very presence make you want to be better. You'll find the beauty, the better, is already within you. Peg it up for the world to see!

Wednesday — March 2

THE Roman emperor/philosopher Marcus Aurelius wrote, "An angry countenance is much against nature."

Is it? What do we see when we see an angry face? Someone who has been hurt, perhaps, and who might relieve themselves of that pain by spreading it around?

But what do we see when we look on a happy face? Someone who has discovered something special, whose spirits are elevated, whose burdens have been lightened and who would happily share.

We can't all wear happy faces every day, but we can take turns and encourage each other. On the days when you can, smile! On the days when you can't, allow yourself to be "infected" by the smiles of others.

Let our nature be encouraging and worth smiling about.

Thursday — March 3

DON'T let opportunity pass you by.
Grab it with both hands and try
To reach that goal within your heart;
Be positive right from the start.
Sow a seed and you never know
Just how much that seed will grow.

Pamela Ramage

Friday — March 4

LATE one evening, during the War of Independence, the American ship *Constitution* dropped anchor outside what was thought to be a safe harbour. Overnight, the wind died away. When the sun rose, the *Constitution's* crew saw five enemy ships staring at them.

Out of sight of the enemy, the captain sent a boat out with the anchor. Those in the boat rowed until they reached the end of the anchor rope and dropped the anchor overboard. The sailors on the ship wound it in, pulling the *Constitution* a rope's length out to sea.

They did this for two days and nights! When the wind picked up, the *Constitution* had a good head start and escaped.

If the problem requires a big solution and you don't have one, try a smaller solution and persevere with it!

Saturday — March 5

LORD BYRON'S "The Bride Of Abydos" is a tale of frustrated love set in Turkey. But there are a few lines we might take to heart even if we don't live in a Turkish palace.

Deciding that their love will be for ever unrequited and the world will be a darker place because of that, the young man urges his beloved to rise above the sadness and be a blessing to the world:

"Be thou the rainbow to the storms of life
The evening beam that smiles the clouds away
And tints tomorrow with prophetic ray."

We might be a rainbow or even a smiling beam, but a "prophetic ray" for tomorrow? Sometimes the best reassurance we can give is the "prophecy" that there will be another day tomorrow.

NICODEMUS was one of the good priests in the Gospels. He had wealth and influence, and a heart that could actually hear Jesus.

A Jewish tradition has it that each time Nicodemus arrived at the temple he had a new mat to sit on, which might speak of self-aggrandisation.

But he also insisted that the "old" mats were given to the poor. That was 365 free mats a year.

As important as he was, he wasn't too important to help.

HATE" is four letters long. So is "Love".

"Lying" has five letters. And so does "Truth".

The word "Enemies" has seven letters, and "Friends" has the same number.

Just as they are equally as easy to write, these opposites are equally as easy to live. And it's our choice to make.

Choose the one that fills your heart in the best possible way!

HAVE you heard of a billet-doux?

During the Thirty Years' War, when French soldiers might sleep in a different town each night, they took their chance, whenever they could, to write home.

The letters from their latest "billet" would hopefully be "sweet". Hence the term "billet-doux".

The practice carried on into peacetime, with many a young lover receiving regular letters, generally of no consequence other than the assurance of undying love.

Of course, the subject doesn't have to be love. It can be gratitude, appreciation or wonder!

In an age when people often claim they don't have time to write letters, might we encourage the return of the short, sweet note – the billet-doux?

Wednesday — March 9

THE William Love Memorial Hall is a community facility in the Ayrshire town of Kilwinning. David tells me that in his childhood it was simply referred to as the Love Memorial, which confused him. He never asked, but he often wondered why love needed a memorial.

These days he understands it was built in memory of William Love, a hero of World War II. It's a touching tribute and still a blessing to the local community.

"But now I understand the importance of love better," David said, "I have a new question. Why aren't there more memorials to it?"

Thursday — March 10

A MAN I much admire told me of a rather serious childhood disappointment.

"At that moment," he said, "something in me broke!" He paused, perhaps recalling the pain.

"It has since been repaired, of course," he added, before explaining the point of the story he was telling.

I am sure it was a fine story. But the point I took away from it was this: our breaks can be repaired!

Friday — March 11

BARBED wire fences are good at keeping people out and animals in. But are they good things?

What led me to wonder was a blue tit sitting happily on the wire, easily avoiding the barbs to either side.

To the horses in the field, the barbs would be annoying when they forgot they were there, but I doubt the horse noticed the fence catch its tail. I doubt it missed the clump of hair left on the barb.

The blue tit noticed, though, and it worked diligently to disentangle what it saw only as nest-building material.

Whether barbed wire fences are good or not isn't the point here. The point is that there is rarely a "bad" or painful situation that something good can't come from. In this case, that good thing will be a cosy bed for eggs and chicks.

THOUGH distance lies between us
And I can't see your face,
Or hold you close and hug you tight,
God gave us, by His grace,

Pure love, which scales the mountains
And soars across the sky,
Freefalling down to patchwork fields
To chase a butterfly.

It zooms along the highway,
Leaves footprints on the shore
And, in an instant, softly lands
Beside your open door.

Love links our hearts together,
Invisible but true,
So you are never far from me
And nor am I from you!

Marian Cleworth

HAVE you heard the Parable of the Choir?

It is the notion that a group of singers can hold one note for an impossibly long time – for as long as it likes, actually. Because individual members can drop out and take a breath before returning.

The rest of the choir will hold the note, each taking a breath when they need to.

In any community venture, it is normal that people will have distractions, fall-outs and other demands on their time, but the work goes on.

If we try to do it all on our own, the work stops when we stop.

So, whether we are singing God's praises, helping people, or whatever – we do so much better as part of the choir!

In his world, community is important.

Monday — March 14

J UST because you like to look on the bright side doesn't mean it's not a tough world out there."

I have had versions of this said to me over the years. Yet I still prefer the sunshine side. Not only does it make the world seem better, I believe it makes our lives better.

It's a belief that Benjamin Franklin seemed to share. He summed it up in these words: "Trouble knocked at the door but, hearing laughter, hurried away."

Tuesday — March 15

T HE weather might have qualified as "stormy". Bins were being blown over and somewhere a shed door was banging.

We have a two-seater rocker in the garden. This was its first experience of such weather. I watched from the doorway as it rocked forwards, then back. Forwards, then back.

The storms of life try to knock us over. We may have to go forward with them a little, but remember to rock back to where you belong. Don't be blown over. Rock forwards and rock back again.

The storms won't last. We will.

Wednesday — March 16

I N the 1952 film "Hans Christian Andersen", Danny Kaye sang the Frank Loesser song, "Inchworm".

After a debate over whether imagination or book learning was most important, he watches a caterpillar "measuring" the diameter of a marigold in its repeated, regular movements while the children are learning their times tables in a repeated, regular chant.

Andersen tells the inchworm that its arithmetical skills will take it far, but suggests stopping awhile to notice the beauty of the flower.

Both options are good, with neither excluding the other.

If you would sow marigold seeds, this is the right time of year. If you would like to learn a new skill to help you get ahead, or work on increasing your imagination and appreciation, it is also the right time of year for that!

Take time to admire beauty and nuture imagination.

Shutterstock.

41

ARE you feeling winter-weary,
Tired of wind and rain?
Seen enough of dark, grey skies
And looked for sun in vain?

Yet just around the corner now
Spring waits to raise her hand,
To touch the earth with light and hope
And smile across the land.

So put away depressing thoughts
And wait a little while,
Look out for buds and soft, green shoots
To brighten every mile.

The days will soon grow longer
The way they've done before,
As just around the corner
The spring returns once more!

Iris Hesselden

WAS fascinated to read about a 2,300-year-old pair of boots which were discovered in the mountains of Mongolia.

They had been preserved in ice for all that time, before being carefully defrosted and put on display.

What struck me most was that they were beautiful!

The upper parts were intricately and colourfully embroidered.

The soles had little squares of tin attached for grip, but they were fixed on in diamond patterns.

What did all that tell me?

It told me that even when life was basic and a constant struggle, human beings still looked for beauty.

It's an innate part of who we are and, seemingly, it always has been.

Saturday — March 19

A **NDY** spent several years working as a picture framer. The frame, he reckons, can be the making of a photo or painting

Sometimes it changes the mood, and sometimes it emphasises a particular aspect of the work held within it.

"I was quite clumsy when I started training," he told me. "I wasted a lot of wood and backings. But my old boss gave me what might have been the best lesson of my life."

My ears pricked up.

"What was it?" I asked.

"He showed me how to reframe my accidents as lessons."

Sunday — March 20

O **SCAR WILDE** once wrote, "Who, being loved, is poor?"

Some of us are surrounded by loving family. For some the source of it might be a pet. Some find it unexpectedly in the kindness of strangers. It comes in different guises and from many directions.

Yet there might be some poor souls who consider themselves completely unloved.

When the Bible talks about God giving his son to us, it says he did so because he loved "the world"! In the face of that sort of love, how can any of us be truly poor?

Monday — March 21

T **HERE'S** a story of a surgeon performing a heart transplant. The new heart was in place, but it would not start beating.

Having tried everything else, the surgeon whispered in the patient's ear. He told her he needed her to tell her heart to beat again.

Seconds later, the heart began to beat.

There are many things in life that stop us in our tracks. We get stuck in those places and other people wonder why we won't move forward. The situation seems resolved, but still we don't move.

Often the only thing left lacking is our own permission to live.

Believe in you, and give yourself all the permissions you need.

Shutterstock.

No-one is truly poor
when they know the
love of a pet.

Tuesday — March 22

I HAD met Susan and Eddie on a path near a park. The first thing I noticed was the large dock leaf Eddie was carrying.

Eddie explained that a nettle had brushed his bare ankle, stinging it. Rubbing his ankle with the dock leaf had soothed the pain.

"You find them growing near the nettles," he explained.

"So," Susan began, "you have a stinger and a healer, and the healer grows near the stinger, like someone organised it?"

I left them to their growing realisation. There are more things "organised" in this world than we could ever comprehend.

Wednesday — March 23

T HOMAS FULLER was a 17th-century churchman and writer. The book which made his name was called "The History Of The Worthies Of England".

Would it be uncharitable of me to suggest that many people might have bought it to see if they were included? Some of those who thought their family "worthies" might have been humbled to read these words within its covers:

"He that has no fools, knaves, nor beggars in his family was begot by a flash of lightning."

Thursday — March 24

M ICHAEL DRAYTON, who lived in the late 16th and early 17th centuries, wrote a poem about two travellers entertaining each other with proverbs.

The first presented a proverb and the second replied with one which contradicted it. Nine proverbs were put forth and each one was promptly confronted by its opposite.

The poet said that the travellers met as fools and parted none the wiser.

His point, I imagine, is that wise men and women don't live their lives by the words of others. They use those proverbs as guidelines, mining them for the good they can find in them. Then, in their own time and place, they apply that good as befits their situation.

Friday — March 25

A T the end of the lengthy chat we were having on that particular day, the man took my hand and said an unusual thing to me.

He said, "Thank you for seeing me".

And I wondered who was talking; who, exactly, was glad to have been seen?

Was it the man, ravaged by the self-destructive path that he had been walking for so long, or the innocent boy that he had once been?

We stop seeing properly, I think, when we see a person as one thing – what they are.

We forget what they once were and have no hope for what they might yet be.

There is always more to see in people than the face they present to the world.

Saturday — March 26

T HERE are a number of people in this world – I am sad to say – who will always dismiss others, seeing them as having no importance.

Perhaps they are right, in a way.

These others might not meet any of the standards society measures success by, but you should never doubt they are in this world for a reason!

In his poem "To A Child – Written In Her Album", the poet William Wordsworth predicts that the child will be a "bright creature".

He also warns her not to scorn her humbler friends.

"Small service is true service while it lasts:
Of humblest Friends, bright Creature! scorn not one:
The Daisy, by the shadow that it casts,
Protects the lingering dew-drop from the Sun."

Each person has a purpose and each person offers a service.

Whether we notice it – and understand it – or not.

Sunday — March 27

IT was an ordinary cross-country race. So why did the social media coverage spread around the world?

Perhaps because, confused by the signage, the lead runner stopped short of the finishing line.

The runner behind him shouted for him to keep going and, eventually, pushed him into running again.

Interviewed afterwards, the second runner was asked why he had helped the other man win.

"He was going to win anyway," he replied.

"But you could have won!" the interviewer insisted.

"What would my mother have thought of that?" the runner asked.

He had as much drive to win as anyone, but he had values laid in place long before he set foot on a running track – by his mother.

Let's take a moment, on Mothering Sunday, to wonder what the world would be like if we based our decisions on what our mothers would think of them. I think it would be a much better place.

Monday — March 28

THE abandoned church is surrounded by a dry-stone dyke, an entrance gate and an exit gate.

An adult could swing a leg over the stone wall and it would be no obstacle for scrambling children. The main gates are easily accessible.

But at some point in its history the wall was deliberately breached. It was built up again, allowing for a three-feet-wide access. The gentle rise on the other side of the gap, which most walkers would have taken in their stride, had three stone steps inlaid.

On either side of this afterthought of a gate is grass. There is no path to it, no path after it, and no explanation as to why it is there. All we can conclude is that, at some point, someone needed the way made easier and someone else made it so.

I like that.

If we leave anything behind after we quit our walk here, may it be signs that we made the path easier for others.

Calligraphy takes its name from the
Greek word for "beautiful writing".

Shutterstock.

Tuesday — March 29

THE baseball season will be getting underway in the United States. An American friend, talking about an honest man he knew, said, "He'll tell the truth, ball or strike."

I didn't understand so he explained it. It seems a "strike" is any pitched ball that passes within the defined hittable area over the plate. A "ball" is any pitch that goes outside of that area. Too many of one is good for one team and too many of the other is good for the other team.

The man he was describing told the truth without regard to whether it helped him or not, but content in the knowledge that the truth, ball or strike, always benefits someone.

Wednesday — March 30

HAVE you ever wanted to do calligraphy? You know, that lovely old-fashioned writing you can only do with a fountain pen or a quill? Perhaps you can.

I have tried it several times and made nothing but a mess each time!

What if I suggested you could do calligraphy without the mess?

The Greek word from which the skill takes its name means "beautiful writing".

May all the words we take the time to commit to paper be beautiful. And may they always bring smiles to the faces of their readers. With no mess!

Thursday — March 31

IT may be an apocryphal story, but that doesn't mean there isn't still some truth to be found in it.

The great Italian tenor Enrico Caruso did a huge amount of charity work during his career, but he also personally supported a large number of needy individuals. While watching him sign a swathe of these cheques, his wife is supposed to have said, "Surely not all of these are deserving."

Caruso, so the tale goes, paused and said, "I am sure you are right, my dear. But can you tell which is and which isn't?"

April

Friday — April 1

IN 1686 the English philosopher and archaeologist John Aubrey referred to April 1 as a "fooles holy day". Why shouldn't fools have a day dedicated to them? Everything else seems to have one. But what was holy about it?

Well, it was long believed that fools had special powers or were closer to God than most. On the other hand, people who were willing to risk all for their faith were often thought – with a certain cautious reverence – to be fools.

Either way, the connection seemed to give the court jester a certain latitude when it came to playing tricks to entertain, and the important job of speaking truth to power. The ruler could never be sure who was speaking, the fool or God, so would listen to unpleasant truths without seeking retribution.

In some ways the more "foolish" the fool, the more they could get away with.

All of which is my take on April Fool's Day. Of course, I might be tricking you!

Saturday — April 2

I HAVE fed goldfish in my time, but I have never prepared dinner for river fish!

In his book "The Compleat Angler", 17th-century fisherman and philosopher Izaak Walton suggests that after a few days of fishing, the fish at a favoured spot might become more cautious and bite less often.

He goes into great detail on how to take a board, cover it with turf, fix worms to the turf until it is almost covered, attach it to a pole and sink it into the river. The he recommends the angler goes home for a few days while the fish feast from his banquet.

Modern ecologists would surely approve, and it is a decent philosophy for a sustainable life. If you take out, also put in!

Sunday — April 3

THE second-hand book shop had a well-stocked "Religion" section. The books ranged from modern paperbacks within easy reach to leather-bound and possibly antique volumes on the higher shelves.

Craning my neck to look up, I made out titles like "An Outline Of Christianity", Fleetwood's "Life Of Christ" and "The Bible Encyclopaedia". But one book stood higher and deeper than the rest.

It was "The Home Preacher", with lessons, sermons and quotes for every day of the year, meant to be worked through at home.

It made complete sense. Home is where we are at our most authentic, often where we are most challenged, and where the example we set has a more lasting effect.

Few of us might aspire towards teaching from the pulpit, but every one of us blessed with a home and a family ought to aim to be a home preacher.

Monday — April 4

VISITING Glamis Castle, I read about touch pieces. Scrofula was an unpleasant illness that could be cured (so people believed) by the touch of a king or queen. People presenting themselves for this "cure" were also given a coin – the touch piece.

It's nonsense, of course, but the combination of help by faith and the practical help the coin brought does seem to me like a good way to go.

Tuesday — April 5

*I*S there a flower more welcome than the daisy,
With pointed petals, delicate and white?
To sit and string a chain of them together
Provides the perfect summer's day delight.

So gardeners, pray, don't frown to find them growing
Amidst your lawns so verdant and so trim;
The Lord has gifted you this decoration
For simple beauty surely pleases him.

Laura Tapper

Wednesday — April 6

LOUIS ARMSTRONG was famous for his trumpet playing, for his duets with Ella Fitzgerald and for his deep, rasping voice. But he was probably most famous for singing "What A Wonderful World".

As inspirational a song as it is, people used to take him to task over it. With all the wars happening, the racism, the poverty and so on, how could he say this world was a wonderful one?

The world wasn't a bad place, he would reply, but how we treated it might be.

It was the same when it came to our relationships with each other.

We only needed to treat each other – and the world – a little kinder.

And what was the secret to doing that? "Love, baby, love!" Isn't that wonderful?

Thursday — April 7

I ALWAYS smile when I walk into Linda's house through the back hall. The old plasterboard in the wall has cracked at an angle and slipped slightly.

She could have gone the traditional route and filled it in, sanded it down, and wallpapered over it.

Instead, she used some of her acrylic paints and turned the crack into a branch, complete with leaves, berries and birds landing on it.

Making something beautiful from something unfortunate is a better reflection of Linda's personality.

Friday — April 8

THE anonymous poet made me smile, even if their work might reasonably be called graffiti.

On the wall of an underpass, I read, *When life gets tough and you're faced with defeat, remember somewhere in the world a flower is popping through tarmac.*

Some think the seeds fall into the cracks then grow, but I have seen more than one flower in a path with the tarmac pushed outwards from beneath, where there had been no crack before.

If a flower can do it . . .

Saturday — April 9

IT'S important to be smart, but not too smart.

A woman was selling watermelons. Her sign said they cost $3 each, or $10 for three. A smart young man smiled at the sign. He bought a watermelon for $3. Then another. Then another.

"I just saved myself a dollar by buying these separately," he said. "You aren't a very good businesswoman!"

"That's what people keep telling me," she replied. "Then I ask them how many watermelons they wanted before they decided to give me a lesson in business. One? None? Enjoy."

Sunday — April 10

CHINESE philosopher Lao Tzu believed it was possible to become a child again. More, he believed it was a two-step process.

The first step required paying more attention to what he called the "passion nature". Perhaps he meant being more impulsive, thinking less about consequences. We might argue whether that was a good thing or not.

But his second step towards becoming a child again, surely none could argue with. It involves being increasingly tender. No matter what the aim, that is surely a step worth taking.

No wonder Jesus taught us to pay more attention to little children!

Monday — April 11

MANY days of the year, the island of Arran off the west coast of Scotland looks like one multi-peaked silhouette. On a clearer day, or getting closer on the ferry as I did, we see the hills are actually separate ranges. And one of those peaks belongs to the Holy Isle in Lamlash Bay!

What sometimes seems flat and all one is actually multi-layered. The island's valleys, smaller islands, hills, paths and people make visiting it a joyous experience.

Likewise, what we think of people can often be dictated by how we look. Make sure you get close enough to people to see any hidden beauties that might be there before deciding you know what they are really like.

Tuesday — April 12

J.M. BARRIE and Robert Louis Stevenson greatly admired each other, but Stevenson died before a meeting was possible.

In "Peter Pan", Barrie wrote of a boy who never wanted to grow up. Stevenson, in "Virginibus Puerisque", wrote that no man was twenty-five for ever and the different ages were there to be savoured.

How might they have got on? Well, I think.

Seemingly opposing ideas are often complementary. The best way to live is, surely, to grow older, as Stevenson would have had it, while keeping your childhood close, as Barrie would have had it.

Grow older, but never grow old.

Wednesday — April 13

THE poet Longfellow said, "Most people would succeed in small things, if they were not troubled with great ambitions."

In other words, some people's gaze is so fixed on the future that they don't see what needs doing right now. Take care of the matters to hand in such a way that you will have achieved many, many other important things by the time you achieve that ambition.

Indeed, your ambition may well be to give the small things the attention they deserve!

Thursday — April 14

I WAS directed to an online "thread" called "The Best Lesson You've Learned". Almost every lesson was a positive one.

Here are some examples:

"The quality of my life improves when the quality of my thinking improves."

"We are the lucky ones. We can use that to create more lucky ones."

"Be nice. It matters."

"I'm still learning".

"Kindness over everything."

Friday — April 15

O N this day in 1795, John "Gentleman" Jackson became the all-England boxing champion.

I know little about boxing, and I have less interest in bare-knuckle boxing, which is what the sport consisted of back then.

But that nickname interested me very much. How do you be a gentleman in that environment? Apparently, it is possible.

Gentleman Jim turned boxing into a respectable, organised, more honest sport. But it was the way he went about his business and the way he treated people throughout his life that prompted admirers to bestow on him the epitaph: "This man ne'er made a foe, ne'er lost a friend."

It seems you can be good and true in any environment.

He never made an enemy? He never lost a friend?

There's something to aspire to!

Saturday — April 16

W HAT do you do," he asked me, "if you've been helping someone and you start to wonder if they're taking advantage of you, then they ask for something else?"

"What did you do?" I asked.

"I asked what the man I wanted to be would do. Would he be smart enough not to be taken advantage of? Or would he be kind enough not to care?

"Then, remembering we live in a world that has too many ways of discouraging us from being kind, I got them what they asked for – with extra thrown in for good measure."

I smiled, not surprised.

"But that's not the end of it," he went on. "The next day I came into some completely unexpected money!"

Wouldn't it be lovely to think we live in a world that rewards outrageous, unreasonable kindness?

"But it doesn't," a voice in my head said.

Unwilling to let that stand unchallenged, another, better voice asked, "When was the last time you put yourself in a position where you'd be qualified to know?"

The joy of reading will stay with you for life.

Shutterstock.

Sunday — April 17

IHAVE wondered why ministers wear dog collars.

I was watching "Songs Of Praise" on television and looking at the white stripe the minister wore across her throat.

White is traditionally the colour of purity. The Bible tells us it isn't the things that go into us that make us impure. It's more likely to be the hate in our hearts and the hurtful words that come out of our mouths.

Imagine if we took that thought more seriously and placed an imaginary white strip across our own throats, so that only pure words could pass from us into the world. How would that affect us?

Would we be able to talk at all? Or would we talk more happily, knowing our words had already passed God's test?

Monday — April 18

IF life gives you lemons," the old saying goes, "make lemonade!"

A friend on holiday bought a pack of green oranges from a roadside stand after being assured they were ripening. But not one of them was fit to eat.

Wasted money? Perhaps. But she looked at the shade of the oranges inside their plastic bag, thought they made an interesting challenge, and painted a beautiful still-life of it.

It isn't about what life gives you. It is about what you make of what life gives you!

Tuesday — April 19

READING is one of my great delights. I have read books to pass time, for pleasure or to learn something new.

I couldn't begin to count how many books I have enjoyed – much less read.

I can trace them all to sitting on my mother's knee by the fireside, sounding out from a book with a word and a picture on each page.

"To learn to read is to light a fire," Victor Hugo wrote, "every syllable that is spelled out is a spark."

The fire still burns!

THERE'S many friends we meet in life
Who brighten up our days,
Yet often there are one or two
Who have such special ways:
Remembering the little things
And showing that they care;
Just calling up to say hello
And let you know they're there,
Or send some cheer – a simple card –
That says a bright hello.
These friends are just like gifts from God,
Beside us as we go.

Judy Jarvie

Thursday — April 21

DID I ever tell you I met the Princess Royal, Princess Anne? She was launching a charity I was involved with. I tried to stay out of the way, but I was presented to her.

She told me I was a very important man!

Why do I mention that? Am I showing off? I hope not.

The point I wanted to make was that I might have been one of the "bosses", but she also said something similar to the cleaners.

When I learned that, my pomposity may have deflated a little, but my respect for her reached a whole new level.

Friday — April 22

CHATTING with other men of letters, Samuel Taylor Coleridge described poetry as "the best words in the best order".

The words we use cost nothing, but they can be expensive if used carelessly.

Wouldn't it be nice if we took the time when talking to put our best words in the best order?

Life would be more peaceful – and more poetic!

THE kerb stones separating the different sections of the new city centre pedestrian area looked weathered and old, like they had been recycled from some other place.

A few of them still carried distinguishing marks left either by the masons who made them or the road builders who fitted them alongside their first pavement.

The meanings of those marks are long gone (except, perhaps, to other stone masons), they are no longer relevant to their situation, and people strolling across the new plaza must look and wonder.

We all leave our mark as we pass through this life, but the world has a way of mixing things up. What we mean to say isn't always what people hear; what we do isn't necessarily right in every situation.

The best way always to be understood – no matter how mixed up things become – is to make your mark a loving one.

Those are understandable and appreciated in any place at any time.

Sunday — April 24

MANY of the larger shopping centres have quiet rooms these days. They are multi-purpose and might be used for soothing children, saying prayers or helping autistic people by blocking out the sights and sounds that can become a sensory overload.

I took a peek inside one the other day. It was painted in soothing colours, there was a comfortable couch and a wicker basket full of folded blankets.

I had only looked in out of curiosity, but I could happily have stayed for a while.

A quiet room, a favourite park bench, an oft-frequented seat in a museum, a boulder by the beach, a bend in the river – we all need places like these in our lives.

If you don't have one, make a point of finding one or creating one. It will repay your effort a thousand times over in peace of mind.

And, of course, Jesus often sought out a quiet place to talk to God, so we would be following the best of examples.

HOW well do you sit in a chair? You might think that a strange question.

Frank William Boreham was an English-born preacher who made his reputation in New Zealand and Australia.

His many books and sermons were well regarded. Of course, your opinion of such thoughts might depend on your religious inclination. He did, however, say at least one thing everyone, religious or not, might privately hope was true.

"Every man has a genius for something or other," he said. "I have a genius for a comfortable armchair and a blazing fire . . . I can talk to my heart's content without seeming garrulous, and, when in the mood, can remain as silent as the Sphinx without appearing sullen."

In which field of endeavour – or relaxation – does your genius lie?

THE friendly tour guide in the stately home showed us a semainier. It looked like a chest of drawers to me. Beautiful, but a chest of drawers.

He explained the name came from the French word for "week". There were seven drawers, one for each day of the week. Monday's clothes were laid in the bottom drawer, presumably by the servants. There was a fresh set of clothes for each day, all the way to the top drawer, where the Sunday best was kept.

"It's where we get the expression 'top drawer' from," he explained. "Of course, every drawer, every day and every set of clothes can't be top drawer. But it's something to aspire to, isn't it?"

I should say so!

HAVE you ever hesitated to be kind for fear of being duped?

William James, the "Father of American Psychology", believed it was necessary for some "saints" of kindness to be taken advantage of. Why? Because only by seeing this, reckoning it unfair and wanting it never to happen again, would enough people join the kindness revolution to truly change the world.

Thursday — April 28

ROBERT doesn't have to look far for his problems. Some he can deal with and some he will have to live with.

Twice a week he boards a bus to wherever. He doesn't leave the bus station at the other end; he just boards the next bus home. His peace is found in hours sitting by a window, watching the scenery.

What made me think of him, other than love and admiration, was this quote from Maya Angelou: "Each person deserves a day away in which no problems are confronted, no solutions searched for."

Friday — April 29

PINNEGAR, in Reginald Arkell's 1950 novel "Old Herbaceous", is the gardener at the local big house. A foundling baby, he grows up to find home and family in the garden and its plants.

Mrs Charteris owns the garden and loves it for its beauty. She and Pinnegar often disagree about what should be planted where, but she usually submits to his expertise. In the same fashion, when a plant seems to be in trouble, Pinnegar would ask the advice of the "First Gardener" and go his way.

I am sure Mrs Arkell (and Pinnegar) agreed with the notion that most of us find out, but which Dorothy Francis Gurney put into words: "One is nearer to God's heart in a garden than anywhere else on earth."

Saturday — April 30

IWATCHED as someone discarded half a sandwich on the promenade. I noticed a seagull sitting atop a lamp-post.

This was his chance for lunch, I thought.

But instead of swooping down, he threw his head back and screeched into the sky. It seemed every gull on the coast descended on the half-eaten sandwich. He got some crumbs, while other birds made off with the crusts and the cheese filling.

"You shouldn't have made all that noise, my friend. You didn't help yourself," I told him.

But maybe his example will help me the next time I feel tempted to make a raucous noise.

May

Sunday — May 1

*THE seeds of love are tiny. They can slip right through your hands.
You don't know when your turn might come, or where, 'til your
seed lands.
It turns itself towards the sun and suddenly you know
That love's implanted in your hearts; you just have to let it grow.
Two separate lives reach out as one. Shoots emerge and before long
Flowers bloom and branches touch, entwined and close and strong.
Each new leaf shines, just like the first, giving shelter from above,
As you lay down roots that anchor you to a life that's built on love.*

Vivien Brown

Monday — May 2

HOW is your diary coming along? Approaching half full? Do you
tell long stories in yours, or just the basic facts?

Keeping a diary is generally agreed to be a good thing. It helps you
remember details and dates, it provides something like a sense of
companionship and, in my humble opinion, it is good for our mental
health.

It's a pastime that has given birth to many a witty one-liner.
Mae West said, "Keep a diary, and some day it will keep you." I
suppose it depends on whose names are in it.

Oscar Wilde never went anywhere without his diary, because "One
should always have something sensational to read on the train."
Mr Wilde was never one to underestimate his own talent!

We can take those with a pinch of salt and have a laugh, but I had
my doubts when I read that a British politician (and enthusiastic
diarist) back in the 40s or 50s had said, "What is more dull than a
discreet diary? One might just as well have a discreet soul."

My only question to that fine gentleman would have been: "What
in the world is the problem with a discreet soul?" Perhaps, had I met
him, I would have been too discreet to mention it.

Tuesday — May 3

THIS time two years ago, Julie had more than her fair share of problems. So her friend Jackie sent her a bouquet of flowers.

Of course, Julie phoned to say thank you and Jackie was pleased they had arrived safely.

"Did you notice the little white flowers I had them sprinkle among the others?" she asked.

Julie looked to the vase and said they were lovely.

"They are lily of the valley," Jackie explained. "The flower of May. The name means 'return to happiness'."

"And did you return to happiness?" I asked Julie when she'd finished telling me about this.

"Eventually," she replied with a smile. "But I took my first step on the way that same day."

Wednesday — May 4

THE two-year-old opened the bedroom door (far too early).
"I here again," she said.

Her tired dad groaned, having returned her to her own bed several times the previous night.

"I so much love you!" she insisted.

He threw the quilt cover back and let her snuggle in.

We met later when he was more awake.

"There's no defence," he told me, "when love walks into the room."

Thursday — May 5

DID you know walnut trees and pear trees are famously slow-growing? In fact, as an old English saying informs us, "Walnuts and pears, you plant for your heirs".

It doesn't really matter what we think of walnuts and pears. The point is we still have them with us. Which means gardeners in days gone by thought enough of the future – and us – to selflessly keep planting them.

What a comforting thought.

Shutterstock.

The beautiful lily of the valley represents a return to happiness.

Friday — May 6

"IT shook me," he said. "I am probably going to have to change some of my opinions after this!"

I had known him for years as a man of strong, verging on unpleasant, opinions. What could have made such an impact?

"You might not have noticed," he said, "but I'm a little cynical."

In fact, I had noticed.

"For the longest time now," he continued, "I've been convinced the world was a desperate place. People, I was sure, were not a patch on what they once were, or what they might be.

"Then I met my newborn grandson. Humanity could not be more perfect. And my hopes have never been higher."

Well, well!

Saturday — May 7

IT was a secluded corner of a small park in the middle of a bustling city. He sat on his bag, looked around, and sighed.

As I came closer, he nodded. I took this as permission to disturb his solitude.

"A prettier view might be nice." I looked at the trees, overgrown bushes and the abandoned park buildings that surrounded us.

By reply, he waved an index finger in the air by his ear. I understood. You could still hear the city, but it was muffled enough that you had to listen for it.

"It's beautiful," he said. "It's peace, and writer Walt Whitman said peace is always beautiful."

Sunday — May 8

HAVE you ever received a kindness from a stranger?

We might be made slightly poorer when people don't make their debts right, but we are enriched beyond measure by the gifts of those who owe us nothing.

When we pray "as we forgive our debtors", remember the things we might be owed are nothing compared to the gifts "our Father" bestows on us for free.

IF you like to have rugs on your floors, you might have noticed that they eventually become a little lumpy.

This might be due to spillages, one part of the rug getting more sun than other parts, or just general wear and tear.

Via the wonderful internet, I found some "treatments" for a lumpy rug.

It was suggested that running a steam iron over it would soften all the fibres and allow them to dry again at the same time, helping restore uniformity.

Laying it outside in the sun might have the same effect. Or you might simply turn the rug around. If it is lumpy from being rolled up, roll it the other way.

Why am I talking about rugs?

Well, it occurred to me that the same treatment, translated for a human, would look like this: a sauna, relaxing in the fresh air and changing our way of thinking about whatever makes us feel "lumpy".

THIS life has many problems,
Some days of tears and frowns,
And like a roller-coaster ride
So many ups and downs.
But don't forget the joyful times
To cherish and to hold,
For some days when the clouds are grey
They comfort and enfold.

And see how nature celebrates
Each season of the year,
The beauty, wonder and the joy
Around us everywhere.
So keep this hope within your heart –
This warm anticipation.
Enjoy the many gifts each day,
For life's a celebration!

Iris Hesselden

Wednesday — May 11

IN the midst of a gathering of friends, I found some of the best and most practical advice I have ever heard.

A younger friend was telling Mary about a chance she had to change her life for the better. But she was hesitant.

Should she or shouldn't she?

In reply, our dear friend dipped a biscuit into her cuppa.

"Opportunities are like this," she began. "If I take the biscuit out at the right time, it will be lovely. But if I wait too long . . ."

She lifted half a biscuit from her cup.

". . . it'll be gone."

Thursday — May 12

TIME and again we are told it's how we react to a situation that determines the outcome.

Psychologists and self-help gurus recommend a pause between the actions and our reactions.

That pause, and what we think in it, is very important.

I know it. I sometimes practise it. But I have never heard it better expressed than in what my neighbour Harry told me.

"A moment of patience in a moment of anger can save you a hundred moments of regret."

Old as we are, Harry and I are still learning – and still growing.

Friday — May 13

I AM in a house surrounded by other houses. At the end of the road is a row of concrete garages. Nothing special.

But in one of those garages is a bagpiper who thinks the cost of renting it for his practices is well worth not annoying the neighbours. The concrete walls do a decent job of muffling the sound.

But I am sitting with the patio doors open. The air has that fresh, clear quality you get after a thunderstorm. The roads are quiet and the pipes sound like they might be valleys away.

And, for a little while, I am in the Highlands!

Opportunities are like
dunking biscuits – make
sure to time them right!

Shutterstock.

Saturday — May 14

K EN is a real help to people in difficult circumstances. Rob would like to be like that.

"But I never know what to do. You seem to know instinctively."

"You think I know what to do?" Ken was surprised. "I never do! People's circumstances are so varied. What I do know how to do is take that first step and trust that something good will happen!"

If we wait until we have all the answers, we will never move forward. Trust!

Sunday — May 15

S HE lifted some cereal from the supermarket shelf. I noticed the hole in the side of the box and said, "That one's been a bit bashed about."

"I noticed that," she said. "That's why I chose it."

She made to walk away, then stopped, looked back over her shoulder and, by way of explanation, added, "I thought I would take it in case no-one else did and it ended up in the bin. I'm a bit like that with people as well."

I didn't have a reply. I was just amazed there were still people like that in this world where perfection is so often expected.

We went about our shopping. And the voice of my Sunday school teacher, rising up from my deepest memories, told me, "Whatever you did for one of the least of these brothers and sisters of mine, you did for me."

Monday — May 16

I T was a light-hearted exchange, but it touched on something deeper.

"You are a profoundly wise man," Ruth told Andy.

"All those years of getting things wrong must have finally paid off!" he replied.

Wisdom doesn't come as a gift; it's earned. Next time you see someone being foolish, don't despair of them. Instead, think of them as a genius in the making.

"ARE you talking to me?" I asked.

The café has ceiling to floor windows and a beautiful view of the estuary. We weren't seated by the windows, but one spacious row back.

We were taking the chance to enjoy the view and I had just asked the Lady Of The House if that was a seal out there, when the woman sitting by the window raised her voice.

I lifted my hand to shut out the glint of the sun off the water and saw her concerned expression.

She had heard my voice, seen me looking towards her and assumed I was talking to her.

The sun behind her made her a silhouette from my point of view. I hadn't been aware she was looking at me, let alone talking to me.

I explained when I realised and we all laughed.

And it made me think. The next time I'm on the edge of an argument, I'll take seeing the other person's point of view much more seriously.

Wednesday — May 18

I HEARD a story of a professor who gave a class of students a yellow balloon each. He asked them to blow their happiness into the balloon and then tie their name tag on to it.

Then he told them to throw the balloons into the air and bat them around for a while.

"Now, find your happiness," he said.

What followed was chaos. People got in each other's way, they tripped over furniture and some balloons were burst. Very few students recovered their own balloon in the time allotted.

Then the professor suggested a different way.

"Pick up the balloon closest to you. Then give it to the person named on the tag."

Two minutes later, everyone had their "happiness" back.

Do you see what he did? He taught his students that if we concentrate on ourselves, very few will end up happy. But if we all set out to do things for others, before too long everyone is happy!

Thursday — May 19

WHEN the cousins get together, they like to catch up because life has taken them in many different directions and they don't meet all that often.

But their best stories and happiest memories come from when they were little and all together on Sundays at Gran's.

"We have very different lives now, "one cousin told me, "but we all have the same foundation, a place we will always be welcome and always know we were part of something bigger."

Grandmothers' love. A place to grow from.

Friday — May 20

THE headstone inscription named the man who lay there, adding "at rest in the field he so often ploughed."

He was the farmer who sold the land to the local council.

It seemed beautifully appropriate, but started me wondering.

There are different sorts of rest. Physical work often prompts a deeper sleep than cerebral work. But if the quality of our eternal rest depended, to some degree, on the work we did in this life, might we plough that furrow a little straighter?

Saturday — May 21

IT'S generally thought that writing was developed as an aid to commerce. Like the letter sent to the merchant Ea-nasir in about 1750 BC, complaining about his inferior copper.

The tablet hardened over the centuries and the complaint is now engraved in stone in the British Museum.

If the businessman who wrote the letter had known this would be how the world remembered him, might he have been tempted to write something else?

Most of our written communications tend to be electronic these days. Ephemeral. How about bucking that trend and writing something on paper or card a reader might think worth preserving?

I will leave it to you to decide which words you use, but I am guessing they won't be complaining ones.

A grandmother's love is an irreplaceable foundation for happy memories.

Shutterstock

*J*UST look at her, all wrapped up in the blanket that I stitched.
She has your eyes; she has my nose. She has us both bewitched.
Quick, let's take a photo; one that we can always keep
To record this precious moment as she lies there fast asleep.
We can put it on the mantelpiece, buy a special frame,
Send copies out to all our friends, with the date and weight and name.
I dream of all the years to come, the cuddles and the fun,
The pride and joy she's going to bring, this tiny little one.
She's soft and sweet and beautiful, a gift from up above.
Our granddaughter's just two days old, but already we're in love.

Vivien Brown

Monday — May 23

I **WAS** having a tough day," she told me. "I knew it was bad because I found myself longing for the library I went to as a child. It's not there any more. I found myself talking about it online and calling it my happy place.

"A woman I only know in passing started telling me all about her happy place, the place that makes her feel she belongs when the world seems determined to make her think she doesn't.

"She ended by telling me her happy place still exists. 'You should come see it,' she said.

"Not only did she understand what I meant by a happy place, but she had one of her own and was willing to share it with others! Suddenly the world seemed a much more loving place."

It's the little things!

Tuesday — May 24

A **PELLES,** a fourth-century Greek painter, had the motto, "Not a day without a painted line".

If you would be an expert at something, or even good at something, you could take worse advice.

Find something you enjoy, then do the equivalent of painting a line every day.

THE Laird o' Dumbiedykes, in Sir Walter Scott's "The Heart Of Midlothian", thinks himself dying. He is in the bedroom reserved for such special occasions. He has summoned the minister, the doctor, and his lawyer.

Having settled some financial matters, he seeks to offer advice to his son, Jock. It is, he admits, wisdom his own father passed to him and which he happily neglected. Thus, he is simply repaying a loan by passing it on the next generation.

Dumbiedykes is a difficult man to respect. But there's a suggestion we might take seriously, even so many years after it was heard and written down.

"Jock," he says, "when ye hae naething else to do, ye may aye be sticking in a tree; it will be growing, Jock, when ye're sleeping!"

In other words, if you can do nothing in the here and now, do something for the future. Or if you can do nothing for yourself, plant a seed of kindness for someone else. It will still be growing long after you have forgotten you planted it.

Words of wisdom are for more than just remembering and passing on. They are for living!

I ALWAYS love this time of year, but right now there's a reason
That the month of May is, for me, such a fascinating season!
I moved here in the wintertime when all was cold and bare,
But then some tiny shoots began appearing here and there.
Just what was planted where, and would it bloom? I didn't know!
And it's been so exciting watching all the flowers grow!
I've crocuses and bluebells and a bright pink peony;
I am thrilled when tulips burgeon, too. What colour will they be?
There's glorious aubrieta – a tumbling lilac spread –
A beautiful camellia has blossomed ruby red!
Beside a bright forsythia a little pieris grows –
I've rose bushes as well and I could hardly wait for those!
So, yes, I'm just delighted by each new shoot that arises –
Each day, it seems, this world just keeps on bringing more surprises!

Emma Canning

FREE passes, making stew, being too old to have to explain bad school reports, new scientific theories, paths through woods, fiddling while Rome burns, family silliness and lighthouses at night.

Rediscovering a stereoscope, answering back, potato crisps in a pub, games that children organise for themselves, confessing weakness to people who can't believe you have any, a rich bass singing voice, the Marx Brothers and cosiness.

These and other pleasures were gathered together by author J.B. Priestley in his 1949 book "Delight".

If you have a pen handy and a piece of paper, there are worse ways to spend a little time than compiling a list of your own.

What, in your life, has brought you delight?

Saturday — May 28

IRREVERENT seventeenth-century poet Claude Le Petit wrote, "The world is full of fools, and he who would not see it should live alone and smash his mirror."

I thought of this as I stood in front of my mirror preparing to shave, cupped a hand and filled it with deodorant instead of shaving foam!

These moments keep me humble.

Sunday — May 29

A RAMBLE on a peaceful sunny day took me down a cobbled lane between a large church and a considerably smaller house. A sign on the gate leading to its back garden told me the house was a home called Kirklee.

It struck me as very appropriate. The lee of a hill, a ship or a church is the sheltered side.

Churches play more roles in society these days than they used to, but one of the core reasons for their existence is to provide help for the needy.

In an ideal world, where the command of Jesus to "love one another" was put into action rather than just read, we would all live in the shelter of the church – in the kirk lee.

WALKING arm in arm after a rain shower meant the Lady Of The House and I stopped.

The gleam off a puddle on the path had momentarily dazzled us.

I muttered something and went to move on. My sweetheart stayed put. Using her free hand as a shade, she looked from the puddle to the sky.

Turning me around, she stood in my shadow.

"We see it in so many ways, don't we? The sun lends its brilliance to a humble puddle, making it blaze, but the sun grows no dimmer.

"There are things we can give away that cost us nothing, like time or kindness, that can make a huge difference to others and leave us undiminished. Perhaps they even make us shine brighter."

"Hmm," I replied.

We joined arms beyond the puddle and walked on, me unreasonably proud that this beautiful and philosophical soul didn't mind too much being seen with me.

Tuesday — May 31

HE was a well-dressed gentleman, not dressed for hopping delicately over a ditch by the roadside to examine a wild rose growing through a hedge.

Yet he did.

I, of course, was more sensibly dressed. I waited until he was out of view then jumped from his footprints, slid and ended up ankle deep in the ditch – from where I had a better view of the rose!

Later that evening, my chores done, the Lady Of The House read me a quote by Ralph Waldo Emerson, the American essayist and philosopher.

She told me he had once declared that flowers were "a proud assertion that a ray of beauty out-values all the utilities of the world."

Who, if only they were fit enough, wouldn't take the chance of falling in a ditch for such a rosy ray? Poor souls, I'd say!

Only, as my sweetheart reminded me, some will do it more gracefully than others.

June

THE many mentions of Granny Austin in Great-aunt Louisa's diaries are testament to how loved the older lady was. But they suggest another side of the Lady Of The House's "saintly" great-aunt.

Little Louisa, it seems, was a test for Granny Austin's patience.

So why, despite too many tellings-off, was Louisa's abiding memory of her grandmother such an adoring one?

"After each visit, as we kissed her goodbye by the hearth-side," Louisa wrote, "she'd remind me of the lesson she had attempted to teach me in such a way that no-one else ever overheard.

"When she finished, she would return her voice to normal volume and say, 'Be good, child. I look forward to seeing you next week!'

"Somehow I was always reassured that she believed I could be good and that I would always be welcome back."

*E*NJOYING *my usual evening walk, I paused to stand a while*
And watch the baby rabbits play – their antics make me smile!
What seemed an empty hedgerow stretched along the winding
    lane,
But as I stood there silently I had to think again!
First came some busy buzzing bees and they were quite intent
On seeking honeysuckle flowers, drawn by their heady scent.
Then from the ivy popped a wren, a tiny perky thing,
And then a blackbird landed, too, and he began to sing
His own sweet song, full-throated, pure, as he was unaware
That I stood listening to the notes that filled the evening air.
The hawthorn swarmed with small black flies and then a ladybird
And several butterflies arrived – I smiled at how absurd
To think this hedgerow void of life; I'd been completely blind!
It teemed, it buzzed, it was alive with life of every kind!

Eileen Hay

Friday — June 3

THERE are friends I know who will welcome me in at any time, and other equally dear friends who like a little notice to tidy.

Assuming you know our house is too busy always to be tidy, the Lady Of The House and I operate on a similar basis to poet Thomas Osborne Davis.

He wrote: "Come in the evening, or come in the morning. Come when you're looked for, or come without warning."

The name of his poem? "The Welcome"!

Saturday — June 4

I TALKED with a kite-flyer this afternoon. He's a big-city man, but he comes to the coast to fly his kites.

There are open spaces in the city where he could do the same, but having to rise above, or pass around, the buildings makes the city winds patchy and turbulent. By the coast, the wind is smoother, more consistent.

It occurred to me that I might have stood in the city or on the coast and felt those differences without even being aware they existed.

Like the flights of kites, our life journeys are shaped and directed by many things we can't see – and might never even suspect are there.

Be like the kite-flyer. Look a little deeper. Look a little higher.

Sunday — June 5

DID you know that pansies take their name from the French word *pensées*, which means "thoughts"?

We could do worse than think about the range of flowers in the world, how there seems to be one for every type of environmental niche, how their relationships with the insect world works, how they came to have so many medicinal properties for us humans.

Almost like they were designed to fit into some worldwide complex design. Part of a divine plan.

Or we might just sit a while and think how pretty they are.

Both ways work.

The word pansy comes from the French for thoughts.

Shutterstock.

Monday — June 6

ENGLISH philosopher Bernard Williams said, "If a June night could talk, it would probably boast it invented romance."

There is undoubtedly something of that about this month.

Of course, boasting isn't something I would normally encourage, but there are some things in life worth being proud of.

Inventing romance might be a bit of a stretch for us mortals, but having, at least the once, partaken of it is well worth crediting to the plus side of our life's ledger.

Tuesday — June 7

THINK of the best days in your life so far – other than the organised ones.

Did you know, when you woke up, how good they were going to be? Have you closed the door on the possibility of more days like that?

I ask because I recently read advice from Mark Twain and fully intend to take it seriously.

"Give every day," he wrote, "the chance to become the most beautiful day of your life!"

Wednesday — June 8

HAVE you chanced your arm recently? I think we all know it means to try your luck, but why "your arm"?

The Butlers and the Fitzgeralds, in 15th-century Ireland, had a feud going on. Eventually, it seemed like the Butlers were going to lose so they took refuge in a cathedral. Respecting the tradition of sanctuary, the leader of the Fitzgeralds told them to come out and make peace.

Suspecting treachery and fearing for their lives, the Butlers stayed where they were. Fitzgerald then had a hole cut in the door. He reached through it, offering the hand of friendship.

With everyone on the other side of the door being desperate and carrying swords, he risked having his arm chopped off. He literally chanced his arm!

Thursday — June 9

THE stones in the dry-stone dyke seemed to have been fitted together any old way until it got to the top-most row. The capping stones were all thin, upright and jammed together.

At some point, something had happened. Stones had been knocked out of the wall, leaving a gap big enough to stick your head through.

Now, for a foot or two in the length of the wall, the capping stones had nothing holding them up. But they were too tightly fitted together to fall!

Gazing at this, I understood. That's what it's like to be surrounded by friends. The very ground might drop away from under your feet, but they won't let you fall!

Friday — June 10

EVERY few months she returns to our neighbourhood, selling household products door to door.

She thanked me, saying that even if I didn't always buy something, I always made her feel welcome.

Some others, it seems, tended towards rudeness and slamming doors. I asked what she did in that circumstance.

"I pray for them as I walk."

"Do you think that helps them?" I asked.

"It helps me," she replied with a smile.

Saturday — June 11

A WOMAN passing by said, "Oh, don't touch!"

The little boy paused in the process of picking up a worm. His mother lifted it from the hot tarmac and placed it on the grass.

"He gets that from me," she explained with a smile.

"And she got it from me," Grandad added.

I don't know about the hygiene of picking up worms, but three generations of looking after the most defenceless of creatures?

I'd say that's a family tradition to be proud of.

CHARLIE and Rose stood under the stars on the night of their 20th anniversary, just like they did on their wedding night.

"We've changed a bit since then," Rose remarked.

"Aye," Charlie agreed.

"Well, at least the stars haven't changed," she said.

"Of course they have," he replied. "They've travelled trillions of miles, not all in the same direction. Some of them might be dead by now, and that's their light from years back only just reaching us."

She reached to where his arms were wrapped around her, prepared to separate them, annoyed at his ruining a romantic moment.

"But I'll tell you what hasn't changed." He held her a little closer to him. "Since the dawn of mankind, some lucky man has held a beautiful woman in his arms as they both gazed at the sky in wonder. What we have: that's eternal."

Rose tells me she leaned back against his chest and decided he'd do until the next anniversary.

"Give thanks to the Lord, for he is good. His love endures for ever." (1 Chronicles 16:34)

I HEARD a story about science-fiction writer Kurt Vonnegut Jr. Seeing him pick up his hat, his wife asked where he was off to.

"To buy an envelope," he replied.

"You're always nipping out for envelopes. You can afford to buy them in bulk, but you only ever buy them one at a time. Think of the time you waste!"

Vonnegut insisted he wasn't wasting time, and he wasn't just buying envelopes. Each time he went out he might say hello to a man on a street corner, or ask a woman what kind of dog that was, or give a thumbs-up to a passing fire engine.

Those little interactions were not a waste of time for him; rather, they were the most important use of his time.

I would find it very difficult to disagree. It's so often the little things, the little human interactions, that are most important.

Tuesday — June 14

"THE tour of the island was nice," Karen told me, "but there weren't many highlights. I thought we'd reached a new low when the guide stopped the bus so we could watch goats cross a stream."

She described how the first goat had approached the water nervously, fell in, and struggled out the far side. The second goat did the same.

The third goat approached the edge, drew himself back, then bounded across without getting wet. The next nine goats all did the same.

"You see!" the guide declared as if this was something he had arranged himself. "The first two didn't know it could be done. The third goat showed the others it could be done. And so they did it!"

Wednesday — June 15

"WHAT do you know about Mrs Allinson?" the Lady Of The House asked me.

"Well, I know that she is very much loved!"

"Oh?" my sweetheart said. "And how do you come to know that?"

"Because I spend time with Mr Allinson."

"Doesn't that make you wonder what people who know me, but not you, know about you?"

It hadn't – up until that moment!

Thursday — June 16

"WHEN Romain Rolland won his Nobel Prize in 1915, it was in tribute to the lofty ideals of his literature and to the "sympathy and love of truth with which he described different types of human beings".

I was struck by his description of a hero: "A hero," he wrote, "is the one who does what he can."

Is that all? But then I thought of all the things we might do, and all the reasons we give for not doing them.

If we actually did all the things we can, would that be heroic? I think it would.

The love we have for each other is evident even to those we do not know.

Shutterstock.

AS school sports days go, this was a fine one. There were the usual sterling efforts, glorious failures, mishaps and celebrations.

My favourite celebration belonged to the lad who came in third in a race. He jumped on to the podium laughing, then he did an excited dance.

While the second- and first-placed children were taking their places, he was waving to everyone and showing them his medal.

Happiness. It's not about what you have; it's about how much you appreciate what you have.

MARY and I were discussing the old saying for when things go terribly wrong. Did they go to "pigs and thistles" or "pigs and whistles"? We weren't sure.

The idea of a farmer neglecting his farm, thistles growing in the crops and the pigs rooting around wherever they like seemed to describe the situation best.

"Of course," my dear friend said, "pigs do love thistles! They eat every bit of them, even pulling them up to eat the roots."

I wasn't sure what connection she was making. Then she explained.

"The more thistles, the happier the pig. The worse it is for the farmer, the better it is for the pig in a way."

There is no situation so bad that someone doesn't benefit from it.

THE Welsh poet and long-time rector of an English church, George Herbert, is often quoted as saying, "He who liveth in hope danceth without music."

The idea of hope being a lifelong dance really appeals to me.

Of course, being a man of God, Herbert's ultimate hope would have been in Jesus Christ.

In 1963, Sydney Carter turned an old English hymn of praise to Jesus into a modern song. What was it called? "Lord Of The Dance".

Faith, hope and dancing! What a joyful combination!

IN 1827, Sir Walter Scott decided to write a history book as he might have told it to his grandson. Called "Tales Of A Grandfather", it was so successful that four other volumes followed.

Praised as collections of history, folk tales and traditions, at least one reviewer thought they were light on morals. Not that they were immoral, but Sir Walter Scott didn't often seem to draw lessons and conclusions from his histories.

It occurs to me that most grandfathers would do the same. Tell the stories to the young ones so traditions aren't forgotten? That's important. Be as faithful to the truth as you can? That's essential. But leave them to draw their own conclusions.

If that sounds a little neglectful, I beg to differ. Telling young ones what to think is so often a waste of time, but if you let them decide for themselves, they will make those decisions and stand by them.

But they will have been guided in making them by the example of the person who told them the story, not by their words.

Tuesday — June 21

PEOPLE can be annoying. Some lie, some delight in being obstructive, some happily bring you down. Should we forgive?

Think on this. They were once babies, and what baby wants more than to be safe and to be loved?

Between then and now, those babies found their safety precarious, often absent. They found damaged versions of love or none at all.

How should we feel towards them, then? If we had similar experiences then we might respond in similar ways. If we experienced better, we might be thankful.

The poet Longfellow wrote, "If we could read the secret history of our enemies, we would find in each man's life sorrow and suffering enough to disarm all hostility."

Understanding. But forgiveness?

In the poem "Gerontion", T.S. Eliot wrote: "After such knowledge, what forgiveness?"

Shall we forgive them for having been broken? Or love the spirit of the baby who lives within them and might be encouraged to the surface.

HARRY inspected the leaves of his hostas. A passing shower had left little beads of crystal-clear rain on them.

He nodded towards them.

"Beautiful, eh?"

"Like diamonds," I replied.

Harry looked at me like he wasn't sure I'd ever amount to anything.

"I've yet to hear of a diamond that could refresh a thirsty plant. I've yet to hear of a parched man who wouldn't swap a bag of diamonds for a drink of these little beauties."

I quickly readjusted my priorities.

"Better than diamonds."

*T*URN *on your senses, unlock the key*
And learn to enjoy what the world has that's free:
The scent of a rose as it opens its flower,
The welcoming peace of an undisturbed hour;
A butterfly flitting, a hard-working bee,
A thrush singing sweet at the top of a tree;
The garden refreshed by a brief, passing shower,
A feeling that nature, like love, has the power
To make the day better than we might have known
And to show, with God's help, that we're never alone.

John Darley

HE tripped on the pavement. Seeing people run to help, I waited. They checked he was OK and sat him up. One man shouted to a waitress from the nearby café, "Can we have a seat to rest him on?"

The café had aluminium tables and seats on the pavement, but she grabbed an indoor seat with cushions.

"I brought a comfortable one," she said.

I lifted my head and thanked God for the kindness of strangers.

Saturday — June 25

IN "A Study In Scarlet", Sherlock Holmes compares the brain to an attic, saying it can only store so many things.

If he wants to remember the important things, he insists, then he must forget some trivial things.

I'm not saying that's how it works, but I'm not saying it's wrong.

I am saying that before we decide we are smarter than someone else, we might wonder what they think is important to know, and if it makes their life, or other people's lives, better.

Sunday — June 26

IF you make scones, you need eggs, caster sugar, baking powder, butter, milk, flour and vanilla extract. I'm sure to have added something or missed something out.

Anyway, there are things on that list which, if I were offered them individually, I would politely decline.

But mixed together by someone who knows what to do, they make beautiful scones.

Our bad days are things we might decline if we had the option, preferring only good days. But imagine they are being mixed together in the right amounts and worked by someone who definitely knows what they are doing . . .

I hope the results will be just as beautiful – if not more so!

Monday — June 27

A SEEKER after wisdom decided to test his teacher. Pointing to a large boulder in a field, he asked the teacher how heavy it was.

"Not heavy at all," was the teacher's reply.

"But, sir," the frustrated student replied, "that boulder could crush both of us!"

"Yes," the teacher replied. "If we tried to pick it up it would be very heavy, but walking on past it, as we are, I do not find it to be heavy at all."

Choose the weights you want to carry. Feel free to walk around the rest.

THE perfumed roses are sweet bliss.
The flowers fill my view:
A mix of peaches, yellows, pinks
In every lovely hue.
I've tended all my special plants,
All nurtured to their prime;
The pay-off's heavenly delight
In sweet rose scent sublime.

Judy Jarvie

Wednesday — June 29

JIM was sitting on a seafront bench. I offered him a penny for his thoughts.

"Today," he said, "my eight-month-old grandson played a game with me that his mother used to play when she was his age.

"And today, my seven-year-old granddaughter phoned to sing me a song her mother sang when she was that age. It made me think."

"Did it make you feel old?" I asked.

"It did," he replied. "That's what's got me puzzled. I never expected feeling old to be so wonderful."

Thursday — June 30

MOST of the gardeners I know allow a share for nature. They sow more seed than necessary, accepting that birds will eat some.

They might prefer the leaves of their plants bitten than put down pest repellents, understanding that gardens should work for both gardener and "pest".

Now we are in cherry season, I would like to offer the 18th-century English writer Joseph Addison's take on living with his own patch of nature.

"I value my garden more," he wrote, "for being full of blackbirds than of cherries, and very frankly give them fruit for their songs."

If we take care of the blackbirds, they will take care of the songs.

July

Friday — July 1

MOST of us will know the expression "Make hay while the sun shines". It prompts us to do things at the right time rather than put them off until later.

In long-ago times, the month of May was known as Thrimilchi, because the grass was so lush and plentiful that farmers had to milk their well-fed cows three times a day, rather than the more usual morning and night.

July was known as Hewi-manod, meaning hay-making, when the grass grown for that purpose was harvested and laid out to dry.

Eventually, if it could be dried before rain spoiled it, it would become the hay that would feed the cattle through the winter months.

Winter is a while away yet, but in farming, as in life, rain, real or metaphorical, is always a possibility. The wet stuff might spoil the hay; the unfortunate or unlucky stuff might spoil our day.

It's always best to be prepared.

Saturday — July 2

HAVE you heard of a "fire of joy", or a "feu de joie"? It's a military term. Imagine a line of solders in their ceremonial uniforms. They raise their rifles and fire into the sky. They shoot one after the other, but so closely following each other that the series of shots sounds like one continuous noise.

Shooting doesn't normally make me joyful, but think about it. From the second in line onwards, each soldier fires after the one before, they pay close attention to each other, they each have a part to play, and if any one of them didn't fire it would be noticeable. The whole group depends on every individual. Each is as important as the next.

It reminded me of the generations of a family. Now isn't that something to be joyful for?

Sunday — July 3

ON this day in 1938, the Mallard broke the speed record for steam engines, achieving 126 miles per hour on the stretch of line between Little Bytham and Essendine.

We seem to have a passion for going faster. Of course, spending less time travelling does have benefits in terms of efficiency.

As in all things, though, let's have a little balance. Travel by the latest, fastest technology when it suits you, but take time, every once in a while, to savour the scenery from on board a slow train.

How you make the journey is often more important than how quickly you get there.

Monday — July 4

TODAY, America celebrates its independence. That reminds me of Margaret, who was married for 60 years to a man who told her the world was an evil place and people were cruel.

Aged almost eighty, she walked out the door with nothing but the clothes she was wearing. What courage!

As I helped her navigate the food bank, she was buzzing with excitement.

"He was wrong, you know," she told me, clutching my arm. "People are so kind!"

Fear and unhappiness – make yourself independent of them!

Tuesday — July 5

A MAN born to wealth was criticised for saying he understood how people living in poverty felt. I didn't doubt his sincerity and good intentions, but could he really know?

Writer and philosopher G.K. Chesterton said, "One sees great things from the valley; only small things from the peak."

From the heights we see the grand views and the eagles, but we miss the fish glinting in the stream, the flower growing from a crack in a rock, the tracks of the deer, the hedgehog in the grass.

A helping pound coin from a friend with little to spare is a treasure the poor millionaire could never buy.

A record-breaking steam train.

National Railway Museum, York.

Shutterstock.

Wednesday — July 6

WHEN Jane Addams won her Nobel Prize in 1931, it was for advancing women's rights and being a peace-builder.

"Peace-builder". Isn't that a wonderful title?

Too many people think peace is a sort of default position, like it's what we have left when annoying people and upsetting situations are removed.

But peace, most often, has to be built. Good people actively make it happen.

Could there be a nobler calling?

We could do worse than ask ourselves, each day, what little thing can I do today that will help build peace?

Thursday — July 7

THE children in the park were laughing and pointing at the inflatables flying above them.

There was a Winnie-the-Pooh trailing a honey pot, Olaf the snowman from "Frozen", and a Buzz Lightyear. They weren't full of helium. Each would have flown in a strong-enough wind, but in a haphazard sort of way.

Looking higher, I saw they were held steady in the sky by smaller plain blue or white kites. And, of course, there was the kite-flyer.

The fun, the excitement and the attention was all somewhere between the kites and the kite-flyer.

Here's to the people who provide safe anchors and the lift that allows others to fly.

Friday — July 8

THE garden had a low stone wall topped by some beautiful black-painted wrought-iron work. The garden looked like it had been well cared for, but was currently a little overgrown.

At some point a branch had grown through an iron curlicue, and a red rose, now bigger than the hole it passed through, had bloomed.

A fence might be an effective way of keeping people out, but it takes more than iron to keep beauty in.

AT this time of the year the plant Diphylleia grayi is still flowering. And their flowers are well worth a closer look.

You see, when the normally white petals get rained on and become wet, they turn completely transparent!

In life, one of our goals should be attaining that level of transparency. It doesn't always work out like that, but the fewer secrets we feel we have to keep, the lighter our emotional burden is.

Find yourself a life, a friend, a faith that enables you to live transparently.

Sunday — July 10

I SAW him counting his pennies at the café till. I told him I would pay for his soup, and why didn't he add a coffee and a cake to his order?

We sat together. He told me he was retired, and had decided to spend the rest of his "working" days handing out religious texts. Or, as he put it, "Working for God."

I said, "It's a shame God doesn't pay a little better."

He finished his sandwich and looked appreciatively at the strawberry tart he chosen.

"Well, I don't know about that," he replied with a smile.

"He just bought me a very nice lunch," he added, "and added a new friend to the order."

Monday — July 11

ROBERT Louis Stevenson, the well-known author of "Treasure Island" and "The Strange Case Of Doctor Jekyll And Mr Hyde", had a talent for words that regularly leaves me . . . well, at a loss for words.

But – and for some reason this delighted me – as a grown man, he called his Skye terrier (among other names) "Waggie"!

Some things are just too obviously right and true that the simplest words to describe them are the best.

Tuesday — July 12

THE broken windows theory is a criminological idea which suggests that people are more likely to vandalise a property with broken windows or act antisocially in that area because it already looks like it doesn't matter to anyone.

But people behave better and less crime is committed in an area that looks well tended.

Caring for the little things – making the place you live in look valued – has a bigger effect than we might imagine.

I must say an extra thank you to Robin, who makes regular trips around the area with a bin bag and a "grabber". Why? For his care, and all the things that didn't happen because of it.

Wednesday — July 13

SOMEONE told me, "The wonderful thing about the wreck of the *Titanic* is that, even after all these years on the ocean bed, its swimming pool is still full of water!"

I opened my mouth to say, "Wow!" Then I realised!

Much more sensible was the comment another friend made about that fine ship.

"It wasn't the billions of tons of water outside the *Titanic* that sank it. It was the few tons that got inside of it!"

When the world seems full of negativity, you'll sail – or swim – better for not taking it on board!

Thursday — July 14

FOUR-YEAR-OLD Blake was excited after his first day at pre-school. "What did you do?" I asked.

"I was a superhero!" he said emphatically. Not seeing any superhero costume on him, I assumed he'd been playing a game.

"How do you do that?" I asked.

"A girl was upset and crying," he explained. "I helped her and she stopped crying. That's what superheroes do. They help people."

If ever you wondered what it takes to be a superhero, take Blake's advice. They help people.

A real superhero helps others.

Shutterstock.

THE new waitress at the café looked somewhat overwhelmed by all she had to learn. As she served Harry, he reassured her she was doing a great job.

After she left, I pointed to the can of fizzy juice she'd left for him.

"She ought to have offered you a glass with that. Or a straw."

"Technicalities," he replied. "She came to the table nervous and unsure. She left smiling and reassured. Which of those two do you think will help her become really good at her job?"

An encouraging word: perhaps even more effective – even more of a precious gift – when not quite deserved.

Saturday — July 16

IN the 1922 book "Tramping With A Poet In The Rockies", the author Stephen Graham begins by saying, "Well, it's good to be going tramping again."

The hills and country paths have different charms at different times of the year, but the July weather might encourage more of us to pull on our boots and venture out.

Vachel Lindsay, the poet of the title, is considered the father of "singing poetry". If you do go tramping, may it be the sort of day that inspires a song, a poem, or simply lifts your heart.

Sunday — July 17

A BUNCH of us were saying our goodbyes and one friend said, "Adieu to you all – even though I don't know what that means!"

It is a late Middle English expression derived from Old French. In a time when journeys were more hazardous than now, your goodbyes might involve commending the traveller and their journey "to God", or "adieu".

In other words, "When I can't take care of you, may God."

It turned out my friend was using the expression in the right way, whether he understood it or not.

Journeys these days might be safer, but may we all commend our friends to God until we meet again.

A BEAUTIFUL voice beneath a high-vaulted ceiling. Magnificent. It is very easy to see why some singers like to do cathedral tours.

Archie told me of his dad, who was a minister of a church in Galloway, and of the lady, a talented soprano, who was doing a fund-raiser at that church the following evening.

As the minister showed the singer around, they both noticed an old shepherd, kneeling at the foot of a grave.

Trying to lighten the atmosphere, the minister asked if the shepherd would be attending the concert.

The shepherd said he wouldn't. Then he added, "But my wife here, she always liked 'Ye Banks And Braes' and 'Ae Fond Kiss'."

A moment of confusion passed, then the singer – bless her heart – sang to an old shepherd's late wife in a church graveyard.

There are different sorts of magnificent performances. This would have been one of the better ones.

N ICE T-shirt," I said. It had a picture of a grizzly bear above the words *Bear With It*.

"I was wearing this when my grandson video-called us," Davie explained. "He liked it and I briefly wondered how I would explain the different meanings of 'bear' to him.

"Later I remembered my Irish granny would have said 'thole it' instead of 'bear it'. I wondered if 'thole' was an Irish word. She had always said the family had Viking roots, so perhaps it was Nordic.

"I was going to call him in Pennsylvania and explain how he had American, Scots, English, Welsh, Irish and Vikings in his ancestry. I thought it through, making sure I hadn't missed anyone out. Then it occurred to me . . .

"I could miss me out! Because I'm his step-grandfather, he and I aren't actually biologically connected.

"I could take Viking out of the mix and tell him my contribution is love. But he's six – that's a terrible swap. So I'll bear it. I'll thole it.

"I'll teach him humanity is his heritage, and that love fights harder than any Viking."

THE skies are bruised and black out there,
With sudden bursts of light.
A storm's been brewing in the air
And it's letting loose tonight.
At times like these, I will not hide
Or cover up my ears;
I go to the window, look outside
And try to face my fears.
It helps me weather stormy days
Of life's hardship or sorrow,
And trust that the peace of golden rays
Will return, perhaps tomorrow.

Annaliza Davis

THOUGHT people would be busy with their own problems. This was mine to fix, so I put off asking."

I heard one person say that.

"I wish I'd known sooner. People rallied around, so we each only did a little, but I think we made a big difference. I'm delighted to have been involved!"

I heard something like this many times from the people who helped solve the problem.

We do ourselves and others a disservice if we believe we can't ask for help. Help someone by letting them help.

IF someone does us a bad turn, it is tempting to strike back, to get even, to reduce ourselves to their level. After all, hate breeds hate.

But if we are willing to accept that, then we must also accept the opposite: that love breeds love. If we accept that, then the ball is back in our court. How should we react?

If we respond in hate, then no-one benefits and things might get worse. If we respond in love, then the possibility of better is most definitely there.

LOOKING back, I was a dour character," Rab told me. "Then I fell off some scaffolding and broke enough bones to keep me off work for eight months. There were times I thought I'd never be back.

"Now I'm just so glad to be up and about that I appreciate everything all the more."

I've heard Rab's story in a hundred guises. No doubt you have, too.

There's a lesson in there for all of us, but it's a painful one.

How about the rest of us just skip the disaster and go straight to the heightened appreciation?

Sunday — July 24

I WAS in the midst of something when our dear friend Mary arrived. Perhaps she saw irritation flit across my face, or perhaps my guilty conscience made it seem so.

After she told me what she had to say, she added, "My plans, such as they are, are my plans. I used to get annoyed if they were interrupted, but then I thought, 'What if those interruptions are God's way of reminding me about his plans?'"

If God was sending a reminder, then Mary is certainly one of his favourite messengers. Maybe I should pay more attention to interruptions. I like the idea of God interrupting my plans with his.

Monday — July 25

ON St James's Day, in times gone by, English children would build "grottos" by the roadside. Often they were hollowed-out mounds of dirt, decorated with seashells and pretty stones.

To attract attention – and a coin of appreciation – they sang variations of this rhyme:

Please remember the grotto; it's only once a year.
Please give me a ha'penny to spend at the village fair.
Father's gone to sea; Mother's gone to fetch him back,
So please remember me.

Times and situations change, but it is never a bad thing to remember the children and put a little more joy into their lives.

Tuesday — July 26

THE picture frame in my hallway holds a stylised painting of a daisy.

Along the stem are the words *No good deed is ever wasted*.

It has been there for about five years. Most days when I am about to leave home, I look at it and wonder what good I might do.

The other thing I think is *"Quod erat demonstrandum", which* is Latin for "So it is proven".

You see, sending me that picture was a good deed. And it has encouraged many more. Even though I have no idea who sent it!

Wednesday — July 27

THERE was a spinning mill in town back then.

It sounded a steam-horn in the morning to waken its workforce, again 10 minutes before the shift was due to begin, again at lunchtime, and again at the end of the shift.

It was heard throughout the town, and in a time when not everyone had a watch, the workforce relied on it. And because it was so accurate, so did everyone else.

It told boys and girls when they were late for school; mothers would tell children which hooter to be home for; businesses would open and close by those blasts.

If anyone would be a "big noise" in any town, may they be one that everyone benefits from.

Thursday — July 28

OUR shoes are a reflection of our personality, or so I've heard said.

Plain shoes, designer shoes, pumps, slippers, cowboy boots, flip-flops, high heels . . . there might be something in the theory.

I thought about this when I heard someone say, "Put yourself in their shoes."

That's all very well and good, but it might help more if we knew why people were in that situation, if we understood what took them to that place, and if we knew why they wore the shoes they do.

SARAH and Jim were starting a new community group. A band sympathetic to their cause offered to play on the first night.

Sarah and Jim planned to cover the band's expenses by passing round a collection bucket. But they forgot.

Realising what had happened, someone they knew offered cash to give to the band.

Sarah was so thankful she put propriety aside and asked, "Are you rich?"

He laughed and replied, "No! Why would you ask that?"

"Because I've seen you help a lot of people like this."

"And that," he told her, "is probably why I'm not rich."

"But you could be if you weren't so kind."

"Ha!" He pressed the money into her hand. "Then I hope I never find out!"

Saturday — July 30

I SAW Bob step out and hand his seven-year-old son a long-handled brush.

"Is he to sweep the whole street?" I asked.

"He's playing frisbee with a friend," Bob explained, "and it landed in a jaggy bush. I could reach over and pick it up for him, but it's part of the game. If you throw it away, you have to recover it."

There's many a good lesson in children's games. And to those of us who haven't thrown a frisbee in a while, remember, if things get jaggy from time to time, take a brush to them and carry on playing!

Sunday — July 31

THE pastor is a showman. His singing is OK. His wife has a beautiful voice, but she's too shy to sing alone.

Together they are sublime. I love listening to them.

It's difficult to imagine anything being greater than God, but you and God? Together in a relationship of love?

You will make music like you never believed possible.

August

HERE'S wisdom that dog walkers and nature lovers will already be aware of.

John Burroughs, the American naturalist, is supposed to have said, "To learn something new, take the path you took yesterday".

I must explain that the path you took yesterday shouldn't, in this instance, be made of tarmac or concrete, but of soil and grass. It may be that your footprints and your dog's pawprints maintain the path.

The path might be the same, but each new time you take it the grass will have grown, seeds might have fallen, trees will have grown and different animals might have crossed it or followed it. Also, new ideas will be gifted to you.

Walk that path with your eyes open and your interest switched on. It will teach you for as long as you are interested in learning.

And August makes a beautiful classroom!

IAM not a brain surgeon or a neuro-scientist, but I am a curious person, so I wondered what the term MNS stood for after reading it.

It stands for "mirror neuron system", a network in our brain which helps us socialise by reflecting the emotions we see in other people's faces on our own.

If we see someone looking sad, we tend to look sad. It helps show empathy, suggests we understand, and is a way of showing the other person's feelings matter to us as well.

Now that I know such a thing exists – now that I have told you how it works – what excuse do we have not to put it to good use?

When people look at you, what emotion would you have them mirror back at you?

The same path in nature is a new experience each day – walk with curiosity!

Shutterstock.

ANNE'S father and husband had a friendly rivalry: a young buck versus the old stag sort of competitiveness. Neither of them wanted to be seen as less macho than the other.

But her dad had a stay in hospital (from which he fully recovered). In the process, he had a tracheotomy, meaning he couldn't speak.

As the family were leaving after a visit, Dad blew a kiss to Anne. Her hubby, thinking it was for him, returned the gesture. Dad laughed the best he could and soon there were kisses being blown all round.

"A man's macho-ness is one thing," Anne told me, "but love and kisses will sweep the floor with it any time!"

Thursday — August 4

ON this date in 1792, Percy Bysshe Shelley was born. He would become one of England's – and the world's – greatest poets.

He is admired for his romantic verses and respected for the philosophies they contain.

But he found no literary fame in his own lifetime. Those philosophies, politically and socially challenging as they were, meant publishers shied away from his work.

History has proven them wrong and the poet right. Some, like Shelley, are so far ahead the world needs to run to catch up with them.

Friday — August 5

ONE of the reasons Vincent Van Gogh's painting "The Starry Night" is so sought after is probably because, at the time, there was nothing else like it.

Vincent, who had his own psychological issues, once described normality as being like a paved road: it was comfortable to walk, but no flowers grew. It's an unfortunate truth. Comfort is fine, except we generally want more of it. And more.

Enjoy it. Try to attain it – within reason. Don't let it be so all-covering it excludes the chance of a beautiful weed, an exotic flower – or a starry night.

Saturday — August 6

A MILITARY jet caught up with a commercial airliner. The jet-pilot then radioed the bigger plane.

"It would be a less boring flight if you could . . ." he began, and then he did a series of spectacular manoeuvres.

"Cool," the commercial pilot agreed, "but can you do this?"

The airliner kept flying, straight and level.

"You didn't do anything!" the jet pilot replied.

The commercial pilot laughed.

"I got up, stretched my legs and fetched a coffee. You youngsters like all the high-adrenaline stuff, but when you get older you appreciate your comforts. It's called SOS: Slower, Older, Smarter."

The "days of glory" are nice, but days of doing what you want, when you want, are nicer!

Sunday — August 7

I HAD so much work to do it was giving me a headache thinking about it," Harry told me. "But I also had a rare chance to take my grandchildren out for the day. I took them out – and my work was so much easier afterwards."

Thinking of this later, I took down a book of quotations and found one wrongly attributed to C.S. Lewis.

"Children are not a distraction from more important work. They are the most important work."

Suffer the little children!

Monday — August 8

I T was a piece of anonymous and deeply philosophical graffiti. Appropriately enough, I found it as I passed from the brightness of the afternoon into the duller light of an underpass.

"We can all be the ones to warm a life with sunshine. Only a special few can be the moonlight in someone's darkest night."

Moonlight and sunshine are the same light. But there are times, of course, when it is more difficult to shine – and more deeply needed.

Tuesday — August 9

ISN'T it funny how words change and a letter lost or added here and there can make such a difference?

In Anglo-Saxon days, a woman who kneaded the dough to bake the bread was known as a "hlaf-dige" or "keeper of the bread".

Someone seeking sustenance would approach the hlaf-dige. She would know what there was, and what there was to spare. She would be thanked with respect if food was forthcoming. That respect is reflected in the modern version of the word.

Begin with "hlaf-dige", drop some letters, keep the "la" and the "di", and you have what became the word and title "Lady".

An honourable title, indeed!

Wednesday — August 10

A WORLD of such infinite variety as ours can be an amazing experience. And yet, for all our love of variety, we are usually more comforted by the things we have in common.

Something was added to that commonality on this day in 1675, when the foundation stone of the Greenwich Observatory was laid. From that came a common time. People around the world set their clocks by Greenwich Mean Time.

"What about those who don't use clocks?" you might ask.

They use the sun, which is what Greenwich uses, so we are still all in time with each other.

Thursday — August 11

IF you are wandering a country lane, you might notice some simple blue flowers with ragged ends to their leaves. These might be chicory or, in German, Weg-wart, the watcher-by-the-way.

In tradition, some whimsical soul had the original chicory be a beautiful young woman, for ever watching the road for her sweetheart's return. She dresses finely and always looks her best – as she would wish him first to see her!

Very romantic. Perhaps a little sexist? But being for ever at your best for love? That's something women and men might aspire to.

HAVE you heard of god-sibs? Does the word seem somehow familiar?

If, in olden days, you invited someone to be a godmother or godfather to your child, then you and they became siblings in God, or god-sibs. Such a relationship was seen as very close.

You were people who could be trusted with each other's secrets. The conversations shared became known, eventually, as gossip.

Imagine if gossip was the same these days: relevant, shared only with those closest to you, and generally for the good of the family.

Saturday — August 13

THE hotel car park was separated from a block of flats by an old brick wall. Unfortunately, someone swung into a parking space without braking and reduced that section of the wall to a pile of bricks.

When the owner of the property didn't seem in any hurry to have the wall repaired, one of the residents arranged them into two short pillars and topped them off with a paving slab.

Two more bricks and a grill-tray from an old cooker and they had a DIY barbecue for the balmy evenings.

Turning negatives into positives is one of humanity's more endearing traits.

Sunday — August 14

IT'S a line from the Book of Romans: "May every soul be subject to the higher powers."

Paul seems to be talking about earthly authorities, suggesting their power was given to them by God. There is much to dispute or debate in that line.

I have to admit I do like being under a higher power. I feel I benefit from having someone who prompts my conscience to ask if I have done my best. Would he, or she, be happy with my efforts?

By "he", of course, I mean God. By "she", of course, I mean his faithful depute, the Lady Of The House.

HAVE you ever seen boxers square up to each other and "trash talk"? Perhaps not. But they do.

And they do it for a good reason. They try to get their opponent angry, because an angry person is an unfocused person.

An angry person is a distracted person. Anger is a weakness that the other man can exploit.

If anger is a weakness in this toughest of sports, it can't be any less in life.

But what about love? Love is strength! Perhaps boxers should begin their bouts by hugging each other.

I can't see that catching on, can you?

Tuesday — August 16

CHARLOTTE BRONTË, author of "Jane Eyre" and eldest of the surviving Brontë sisters, was an optimist.

Why do I say that when I have never read a biography of her? As no student of her life, all I can base my opinion on is her poem called "Life".

In it, she says, "Oft a little morning rain foretells a pleasant day."

Don't let a poor start put you off! Believe it will be better, and it almost always is.

Wednesday — August 17

RATTLESNAKES, for me, are denizens of cowboy films. I have, thankfully, never met one in person.

But I hear that if one is cornered it will become so aggressive (or defensive) that it might actually bite itself in its need to attack.

Sadly, humans do something similar. I know of cases where people held grudges long after the other person had forgotten whatever the incident was, which is like poisoning yourself for no reason.

Don't do things that hurt others. But, more importantly, don't hurt yourself just to prove a point.

The point might slip away while the venom remains.

YOU brought us through the winter, Lord,
And through the joy of spring,
Now help us to rejoice once more
In all each day can bring.

The woods and fields are full of life,
There's colour everywhere,
And so much summer beauty, Lord,
For all of us to share.

The cottage gardens are ablaze,
The days are long and light,
And we are grateful once again
You make our world so bright.

Be close to us when summer fades
And autumn comes along,
And help us keep within our hearts
A joyful summer song.

Iris Hesselden

A TALE is told of Oliver Goldsmith, the 18th-century Irish novelist, playwright and poet, who was playing cards with a friend one afternoon.

A woman was singing ballads on the street outside the house where they played.

In the midst of a game, Goldsmith suddenly left the table and went to her.

When he returned, the others asked him what he had been doing.

Equally as surprised, he asked if they had not heard the grief and the need in her voice.

The had all heard her sing, but only he had heard her distress – and gone to help her.

Be not simply a hearer. Be a listener.

The kind of place where God might go on holiday.

Shutterstock.

Saturday — August 20

SARAH has a worry bag. It's not real – but the effects are.

"Whenever I need to do something I haven't done before," she told me, "I identify my worries. All of them – every one of the things I think might go wrong.

"Then I imagine myself putting them in a floral carpet bag and laying it to one side while I do what needs to be done.

"Then I don't think about them because they are 'over there'.

"When I look in it again afterwards," she finishes, "it's generally empty!"

Sunday — August 21

FOR some, the church is God's home. In Denmark, there is a beautiful coastal town called Gudjhem (God's home).

Along the banks of the River Esk in the Scottish Borders sits the town of Langholm.

I sat on a hillside there one summer afternoon.

This must be where God goes on holiday when he's tired of heaven, I thought.

Let's face it, all of Creation is his. His choice of amazing places to "live".

How wonderful is it, then, that one of his favourite dwelling places seems to be in your heart?

Monday — August 22

*A*T first the clouds turn violet,
The blue sky starts to fade,
Colour fountains stream above,
Soft streaks of pink-gold shades.
In time the sun sinks lower,
An orange sky glows bright,
Then slowly turns a deep, dark red
Till purple skies bring night.

Lily Christie

LETTER-WRITING is seen by some people as a dying art. Please don't let it go!

Aaron Hill, an eighteenth-century English poet, inscribed the following on a window-pane while visiting Scotland:

"Letters from absent friends extinguish fear, unite division, and draw distance near."

It sounds like he had more on his mind than simple homesickness, and a letter would be his wished-for cure!

What might we achieve with a thoughtful note?

Wednesday — August 24

NEIL'S four-year-old daughter was painting a picture of "Home". Thinking it looked lovely, Neil asked, "Is that it finished?"

"No, Daddy," she replied. "It needs one more thing. A rainbow to keep the dinosaurs out."

"On the one hand," Neil told me, "I was sad that, at four, she thought a home needed to be defended. On the other hand, I was glad she chose a rainbow to do the job.

"How nice would it be if we protected our homes with the attributes of the rainbow – beauty, love and hope?"

I haven't seen a dinosaur in ages. Proof, I'd say, that the rainbows are working.

Thursday — August 25

WHEN Samuel Johnson was awarded a pension from the King, he declared he could find no words in the English language to express his appreciation. This was despite the fact that he had written a dictionary of the English language!

Resorting to French, Johnson described himself as *pénétré* by His Majesty's kindness. It means penetrated, invaded, steeped, soaked.

To have it permeate your very being – that's how gratitude feels at its best. Has there been a kindness in your life that has left you feeling that way?

Friday — August 26

I **DREAMED** I died. St Peter checked his book and my name wasn't on the list. He was apologetic, but . . .

Wondering what to do next, I walked to where a mountain path broke through the heavenly clouds.

This was the path all souls climbed to get to heaven, and it was arduous.

I sat on a rock. When the next person arrived, I congratulated them. And the next one. And the next one.

I realised that it wouldn't be a bad way to spend eternity – appreciating people's efforts and congratulating them.

Not a bad way to spend a life, either!

Saturday — August 27

IN his "Idylls Of The King", Tennyson wrote, "It is the little rift within the lute that by and by will make the music mute, and, ever widening, will slowly silence all."

The big thought or the kind act won't always come from the strong and powerful. Usually, they come from humbler sources.

And, if that source will but hold their ground, the usual "big noises" will be silenced in their presence.

Sometimes it comes from the mouths of babes. And older and "wiser" folks smile silently.

Sunday — August 28

THE hymn "The Ninety And Nine" has been sung around the world by vocalists and choirs. It was promoted by Ira D. Sankey, and was a favourite of missionary Eric Liddell.

It refers to the Biblical promise that Jesus will search out and save every lost sheep.

Sound very "churchy"?

It was written in the 1870s by Elizabeth C. Clephane, an Edinburgh woman missing her brother in faraway Canada.

The church is always at its best when it connects the spiritual to our ordinary lives and when it lives in our homes.

As the shepherd searches for the lost sheep, we all search for those we miss.

Shutterstock.…

Monday — August 29

IT was a throw-away comment between friends.

"You should write a book of your life!" There followed some hilarity and a discussion on whether it would be a horror story or a comedy.

Writing our autobiography might be more of a project than most of us are ready to take on, but make no mistake, we write the story of our lives in the things we say and do every single day.

And, whatever genre it started off as, it is never too late to turn it into a love story.

Tuesday — August 30

WE met with a foundation to discuss setting up a food bank. A vote was taken. I voted "No".

The foundation man asked why.

I admitted it was fear: fear that one evening a hungry family would knock on the door and we would turn them away because the shelves were empty.

"It will never happen," he said. "Your donors will make sure it doesn't. People are wonderful, you see."

I'm glad I was outvoted. Fifteen years later that fear still hasn't come true.

Wednesday — August 31

I GUESSED he was differently blessed, even from the other side of the road.

We waited for a gap in the traffic, then walked. Near the middle of the road, he looked up and smiled.

It was a punch to the heart! I was in tears before reaching the far pavement.

Why? Because I had never been on the receiving end of a smile so pure and guileless.

What could I have said to him? Nothing. He was on his way, anyway. But it does me the world of good, in difficult times, to remember that such God-filled smiles are out there!

September

I USUALLY know better than to offer the younger generation advice. It's a fact of life that lessons learned by living them are the best kind. Everything else is words, and words are easily forgotten.

Having said that, if I thought any advice of mine would make a difference, I would offer this – sow love! I have learned that we reap what we sow. The things we sow before we know any better will come back to us. We don't need to be bound by them, but we will see them again.

The best way to have a gentler old age is to sow love while we are young. We mostly ignore such advice, but sometimes we have good examples who make a difference.

In what is traditionally the month of reaping, may your harvest be plentiful!

J OSEPH BÉCARD was a servant in a grand house before the French Revolution. After the revolution, he worked the streets of Paris, buying old clothes and selling them on for a pitiable profit.

This is where he met Madame Chavilliac again. She had been a frequent visitor to the grand house and had always treated him well. Now she was widowed, destitute and ill.

Bécard had little to offer, but he took her in, fed and cared for her for the next 11 years. By the time she died, he had given up his work to care for her full time, carved her wooden cross and was the only mourner at her funeral.

Where did he have to go from there?

Well, the Academy of France heard his story. They facilitated the de Montyon Prize for Virtue. They awarded Bécard first prize – and 1,500 francs!

Virtue is its own reward, but a small fortune doesn't hurt!

Saturday — September 3

IN Britain, on this day in 1752, nothing happened. Nothing also happened on the 10 following days.

It wasn't that the country was extraordinarily peaceful. It was a change of calendar that meant the third of September automatically became the fourteenth!

Apparently some people protested, demanding they be given their 11 days back.

What would they have done with them, I wonder. Would they have partied, or lived finer lives on those supposedly precious days?

The only day that matters, of course, is today. It is the day we live our lives in. So if ever there was a time to live better, do better, love better, it is this one.

Regardless of what the calendars say.

Sunday — September 4

IMAGINE you could debunk God," I said. "Prove faith was a crutch and prayer made no difference. How would you explain love?"

"Easy," he replied. "It is a chemical trick played on us by nature to ensure survival of the species."

"What about sacrificial love? Jesus said the greatest love was when a man laid down his life for his brother.

"If the man is fitter, stronger, more capable than his brother, more of an asset to the species, and still he dies in his brother's place, how, then, do you explain love?"

"I don't know," he had the grace to say.

I don't know, either, but they tell me God is love.

Monday — September 5

AN old Arabian proverb says that, "The heart will grieve over what it has lost; the spirit rejoices over what it has left".

You won't often hear me talking about over-ruling the heart. Indeed, grieving is a healthy, necessary process we all must go through. But don't ignore your soul, and try hard not to let loss, awful though it may be, overwhelm all the blessings you have left.

THESE tiny country churches
Mean such a lot to me –
They seem like small lighthouses
In life's often stormy sea.

Their doors are always open –
I often slip inside
And spend a quiet moment
When cares can all subside.

The ancient peace engulfs me
And fills my soul with calm
As those who've gone before me
Have felt the healing balm.

Eileen Hay

Wednesday — September 7

I WAS talking to a neighbour about the impending collapse of civilisation. He laughed! Then he apologised.

"I'm sorry," he said. "But you're talking to a gardener. We deal with 'the collapse' every year around this time.

"And what do we do? We start preparing our little corner of 'civilisation' so it stands the best chance of growing again when the time comes."

Might the world be in a better state if anyone wanting to be a politician trained first as a gardener?

Thursday — September 8

BOLIVIA'S Salar de Uyini is a salt plain that covers around 4,000 square miles of completely flat terrain.

At certain times of the year a nearby lake will overflow, covering the plain with an inch or so of water. It becomes a mirror, reflecting the vast Bolivian sky. It is known as "When Heaven Meets Earth".

It must be a breathtaking experience and I would love to visit, but actually, Heaven meets the earth all around the world, many times a day, when one person reaches out to another in love and kindness.

Friday — September 9

MOST street names will be duplicated somewhere in the country. There are just so many thoroughfares needing names.

But if you type "Gran Street" into a search engine, you will find just one – in Clydebank.

The story goes that the houses there were built after the war for retired folk, most of whom would have been grandfathers or grandmothers, so the local council called the place Gran Street.

I'm not sure how true the story is, but it would be a lovely tribute, and the very least that grandparents everywhere deserve!

Saturday — September 10

ALISON posted a picture of her beautiful baby on social media. There was a sign saying, "Today, I am one week old!"

Seven days later, there was another one. It said, "Today, I am two weeks old!"

A week had passed. Was that really worth a celebration? Alison thought so. A week for a new baby is usually a tremendous period of growth and learning.

We lose the enthusiasm for celebrating weeks after we have known a few hundred (or thousand) of them, but they themselves are no less an opportunity for development and learning.

How much they are worth celebrating depends entirely on what we do with them.

Sunday — September 11

WE find comfort in being with people like us. But how far can we take that before we find ourselves not needing "the other", before we find ourselves stifling growth?

"God creates difference," Rabbi Jonathan Sacks said, "therefore it is in one-who-is-different that we meet God. Abraham encounters God when he invites three strangers into his tent."

We tend to praise diversity in every other aspect of creation. May we appreciate wonderful variety more in God's favourite creation – us. All of us.

MAYA ANGELOU'S life began in the south of the United States, surrounded by poverty and abuse.

By the time she died she had received around 50 honorary degrees, written three autobiographies, poetry, television shows, plays and films.

How? Well, it wasn't easy but, as she explained, "I decided . . . to invent myself. I had obviously been invented by someone else – by a whole society – and I didn't like their invention."

In younger years, we are usually composed of other people's ideas and influences, but if you were to invent yourself, who would you be?

HOW much do some people talk? How many of their words are useful?

Of course, our words do not always have to be informative; sometimes a little harmless chatter can be a bonding thing.

Talking can be excellent therapy. But far too high a proportion of our words are used to get one over on someone, to protect a wrong thing or simply to deceive.

Can you imagine the difference it would make to the world if we took this advice credited to Saint Augustine and only said good, positive, reinforcing things?

"Words were not meant for men to deceive amongst themselves, but for everyone to pass on to others the goodness of their own thoughts."

WE might say of them, "They are a couple", and the phrase will imply so much more than that there are two of them. In that example, "a couple" is so much more than the sum of its parts.

Thinking along similar lines, G.K. Chesterton wrote, "Two is not twice one; two is a thousand times one."

Be with the one who not only adds to your life, but multiplies it!

O N this day in 1784, a young Italian called Vincenzo Lunardi amazed the people of England – or those people able to get to the Artillery Ground in Moorfields – by performing that country's first manned balloon flight.

The crowds were amazed by the "miracle" they witnessed. Lunardi performed the same feat all across Europe. His fame was such that people bought a whole variety of souvenirs bearing his name and likeness, providing money for more adventures.

Balloons are no longer our primary means of flight, but would powered flying machines have come about if young Vincenzo (and others) hadn't risen into the air like a dream whose time has come?

It isn't necessary that we get everything the best it can possibly be at the first attempt. Often all that's needed is for someone to move beyond what the world previously thought was impossible.

Friday — September 16

I HAVE often seen beautiful poetry or startling philosophies attributed to fourteenth-century Persian poet Hafiz.

Looking for more information on him recently, I discovered another spelling of his name: "Hafez", which translates as "the memoriser" or "the safe-keeper".

To remember the moments and the people of your life, present them to the world "dressed" in their very best clothes: that would seem like a life well spent to me.

Saturday — September 17

W ERE you a Boy Scout or a Girl Guide? The founders of these organisations would have merited impressive memorials when they died. Indeed, the government offered Lady Baden-Powell space in Westminster Abbey for her husband's tomb.

Both now lie beneath a simple headstone in Kenya. Other than their names and dates, the stone bears the symbols of the Scouts and the Guides. There is also an engraved circle with a dot in the centre.

Scouts or Guides who remember their trail signs will know what that means: "Gone home."

Shutterstock.

Hot-air balloons paved the way for human flight.

Sunday — September 18

THERE is an old story of two men of different faiths arguing over religion. In particular, they were arguing over the nature of the church.

"I tell you," the first man insisted, "my church is *the* church!"

"Away with you!" the second man said. "Go fill your bathtub and tell me it's the whole of the ocean!"

At the risk of offending everyone, might I suggest that the church is likely to be much bigger and far more wonderful than any of us suspect?

Monday — September 19

SOME of my older friends still have their childhood autograph books.

Not the kind used for collecting celebrity signatures, but for collecting names of friends, family, visitors: people they would care to remember.

Often, the signatories would add a few words of advice, or a wish for the book's owner.

If I handed you a blank sheet of paper, suggested we might not meet again, and asked you to write something I could remember you by, what would you write?

It might be wisdom passed on to you, it might be something learned by experience. But if you had to sum up your philosophy for life in a few words, what would those words be?

It's a thought, isn't it?

Tuesday — September 20

SHE had asked me for help so often that I began to suspect she was taking advantage of my good nature. Then she asked again.

I braced myself to say "No". I prepared to tell her what I thought of her. Surely she would take a telling and turn her ways around.

Did I care? Well, I care about the example I set more than I care about my dignity. So I gave her what she wanted – and more. As I have been given.

THE little bird was tangled in a weighted fishing line. Its squeals were bound to alert the hawks who nested in the nearby trees.

It struggled to get away, but the fingers of one hand enclosed it like a gentle cage. It panicked for about 30 seconds, then it stopped, seemingly reconciled to its fate. With my other hand I gradually undid knots and tangles until the fishing line fell away.

I opened my hand. The bird lay still for a few seconds. Then it gave itself a shake and it flew away. Free!

I think of that bird when I feel trapped by circumstances – when nothing I can do will make a difference, I trust that someone, somewhere, is working away on my behalf.

THE autumn equinox is the first official day of autumn. The days will get shorter, the nights longer. As the northern hemisphere leans away from the sun, our world becomes a dark place. But only for half the year.

As it is with the world, so it seems with our lives: a seemingly equal number of good things and bad.

We can do nothing about the axial tilt of the world, or the hours of direct sunlight the country gets. All we can control, it seems, is the amount of sunshine we personally put out.

As autumn begins, can I ask a favour? For everyone's sake, please shine!

THE band had performed a rousing set.

Amidst a standing ovation, the singer said, "Thank you for allowing us to play for you. Take care of yourselves." She paused then added, "And those around you."

Those first four words mean one thing, but the last four change that meaning. If only we lived in a world where we could focus on taking care of others, knowing others would help take care of us.

We could – if enough people were willing to take the chance.

Saturday — September 24

THE Lady Of The House put Great-aunt Louisa's diary on her lap and sighed.

Of course, I asked.

She reminded me that Louisa's family had been fairly well to do, then she read to me:

I felt slightly nervous about questioning Mother's ways. She had asked Mrs Williams, the widow next door, if she might borrow some salt. But we had an unopened box in the pantry.

"I asked for a little thing because she is in need," Mother told me.

I was thoroughly confused. That seemed to make no sense.

"She has borrowed from us already and was embarrassed to do so," Mother explained. "I did this so she might think us equal in our difficulties and feel free to ask again whenever the need arises."

Sunday — September 25

GEORGE is a retired minister and a friend. As well as helping with his congregation's problems all these years, he has lived through a series of personal traumas.

I suggested it was more than any man could be expected to bear and asked how he found the strength. He pointed to his Bible and said, "The answer's in there."

"Something Jesus said?" I ventured.

"No," he said. "My strength comes from the number of times it says, "It came to pass". Never once did it say, "It came to stay". We can deal with anything if we know we only have to outlast it."

Monday — September 26

I HAVE many friends who indulge in a little embroidery. I have one who indulges in "profane embroidery".

If something upsets her, she gets her threads and frame out and, as carefully as she can, she embroiders her frustrations on to the cloth.

The focus becomes a meditation and getting the words out her head leaves space for happier things.

Making ugly thoughts beautiful as a therapy? It seems to work!

A therapeutic
hobby for
frustrated
thoughts?

Shutterstock.

HEARING he could do it, I asked eight-month-old Oscar for a high-five.

I held up my hand and he reached towards it. My hopes got high.

Then he tickled my palm, giggled, and buried his face in his mother's shoulder.

I tried again. Once again, his fingertips fairy-kissed my palm and he laughed out loud before hiding again.

We went for third time lucky and Oscar almost fell out his mum's arms laughing at my confusion as he "tricked" me one last time.

Who knows what goes on in a baby's mind? But when they are entertained they are completely entertained.

And it's infectious – I was delighted! His mum was delighted, too. Why? Only Oscar knew, but that was enough!

Wednesday — September 28

IF the number of bees in a hive drop at this time of year, bee-keepers are not surprised.

It happens as a natural part of the bee life cycle.

If all bees were to disappear, that would be a serious problem!

In times gone by, if there was a major event in the family, like a birth or a death, someone would be sent to tell it to the bees.

They might knock gently on the hive before relating the news.

If bad news was being reported, it would generally be followed by a plea for the bees not to leave. Because that would make a bad situation infinitely worse.

Could you imagine talking to a beehive about your work, or your grandchild's health, or the son you hadn't heard from for a while?

It would have something of the confessional about it, wouldn't it; something of talking to God? Telling the bees probably soothed many a troubled soul.

I don't know if anyone understands how the tradition came about.

Foolish or not, isn't sharing the details of our lives a wonderful way of showing our understanding of how interconnected we all are?

A **PAIN** in my kidney sent me to hospital. They kept me in overnight while they ran tests.

That evening, a young man was admitted.

I heard him crying in the middle of the night, so I sat beside him. We talked quietly for hours about what he'd done, the pressure he'd been under, how he had let his mum down (the cause of his tears) and how mother's love was the next thing to God's love.

I assured him forgiveness would be forthcoming. He went to sleep, much comforted.

Next morning, I spoke with his mum, then she hugged her son.

My tests came back negative. The doctors questioned why I was even there.

I think I may have been pushed there by the finger of God. Why? Well, because I felt it. Where? Right there in my kidney.

A LL colours of the rainbow are gathered round my wrist:
Yellow as the sunshine breaking through the morning mist;
Oceans of deep blue and green and shores of golden sand;
Pink for sun-washed dawns and purest white for snowy land.

All colours of humanity share this great world of ours:
Whatever race, whatever creed, poor or superpower,
Every person's different, yet every one the same,
Each of us an equal, no matter what our name.

All colours of the universe bring richness to the soul,
Each in splendid contrast, each shade adding to the whole.
Unique in its own beauty, but a necessary part
Of God's tapestry of nature – the same with every heart . . .

So be yourself – don't be afraid to let your talents blaze;
Use those precious gifts of yours to cheer another's day.
The friend who made my bracelet, threading beads on finest twine
In all colours of creation, surely brightened mine!

Marian Cleworth

October

I **SUPPOSE** he'd a right to complain about them forgetting his coffee. At the same time, I saw another customer rise, steady himself with the back of his chair and stand there.

A waitress walked to him and took a banknote from his hand. She paid for his lunch at the till, returned with his change, then offered him her arm.

Together they shuffled out to the car park, where she saw him into the taxi the café had organised for him. Then she ran back to work.

The coffee-deprived man was still complaining about terrible service. He had a right, but a wider look around might have softened his ire.

WE thank you for the harvest, Lord,
The gifts that you bestow:
The springtime sun and summer rain
That help the plants to grow.
We thank you for the fruit and grain
For all of us to share;
Now help us reach out far and wide
And show the world we care.

We thank you for the beauty, Lord,
This special season brings,
And for the bounty and the joy
That help our hopes take wings.
So many blessings all around,
Remind us every day,
And let the harvest touch our lives
And light our future way.

Iris Hesselden

TOBY had loaned me his favourite book – and I lost it! Time passed and neither of us mentioned its absence.

Fifteen years later, I found it down the back of the bookcase.

Knowing he was going to be at a gathering, I wrapped the book up and took it along, armed with my most humble apologies.

"Oh, my!" he exclaimed, opening the parcel. "Oh, my!"

He shook my hand enthusiastically.

"Thank you for giving me the pleasure of being reunited with an old friend!"

Some people accept apologies gracelessly, some as their due, but some special individuals make your apology seem like you did them a favour!

Tuesday — October 4

A FEW of our problems are actually serious. Most of them just seem so to us.

Today was a dreich day – dull, wet, dismal. But before I locked up for the night, I stepped outside and, through a sizeable hole in the clouds, I saw Mars.

I realised, like many of the earth-shaking problems we think we have, our weather is purely local.

These things are hardly even noticed by the Martians.

Wednesday — October 5

I HEAR there was a tradition in warmer countries, in times gone by, to insert cobbles with dips in them at intervals along roads and pathways.

The dips gathered the rains or the morning dew and provided a cooling drink for birds or the street animals. People might step over the concave cobbles, not even noticing they were there.

It doesn't take much to help, does it? A little thought by the stonemason, or whomever was paying for the road, and thirsty creatures had a drink. If you are concerned enough to help even the smallest and the neglected, you will always find a way.

Thursday — October 6

CERTAIN times of the year have a special feel to them, don't you think? Sometimes you experience that feeling without being particularly aware of it.

Canadian poet Francis Sherman wrote a poem called "October". I don't want to share it all with you, good as it is. Just two words.

The poem begins with the words "October's peace." I read this and realised that this is the feeling the month of October brings. Peace!

May you enjoy it as I intend to!

Friday — October 7

SPEAKER after speaker at Sandy's retiral party mentioned his helpfulness.

Before mobile phones, I was trying to put a phone extension by the bed of a lady who was ill and might need to call for help. Try as I might, I couldn't get it to work!

Sandy used to be a telephone engineer, so I gave him a call. I began by asking how his day was.

"So busy," he replied. "How are you?"

I explained what I was doing, hoping for some advice.

A moment later, despite being busy, he said the wonderful words: "I'll be right round!" He had everything sorted within minutes.

People like Sandy make the world a kinder and more beautiful place.

Saturday — October 8

PET names for loved ones are many and various, but they do add more than a little to the charm of life.

The politician Charles Stewart Parnell addressed Kittie O'Shea as "My dearest wifie", despite him being married to someone else!

One pet name (for a lady I know well) came when she was cuddling her husband at night and said "Sweet dreams".

He had an epiphany and realised that she was his sweetest dream, so he addressed her as such in every letter he wrote to her after that.

Sunday — October 9

SHE had left her walking frame at the end of the pew while she worshipped.

I looked at it from a mechanical point of view, seeing how it opened and closed, how the brakes worked.

When I had finished with that "man stuff", I saw the protective pads.

The frame was sturdy and strong, as it needed to be, but a leg bumping against that strength could be bruised – hence the pads.

May we be granted the strength to be a support to others. But may that strength always be tempered with tenderness and protection so we don't cause more problems.

Monday — October 10

MABEL is the Samoan mother of three boys and three girls. We met while she and her husband Jason were taking the children on a tour of Europe.

She said something in passing that I have shared with other families dealing with different problems.

"Families don't have to be perfect," she said. "They just have to be united."

With each other? With other families? Either works. And both are good.

Tuesday — October 11

I READ poetry when I'm stuck," Sheila told me. "When I can't see how to get a thing done or when life has beaten me down to a place where I can't be bothered any more, I read my favourite poems, or take a chance on new ones."

"Do you find the answers in the poems?" I asked.

"Never." She smiled.

"Then why?"

"Because they raise my spirits, they fill me up, they remind me what is important and they restore me. Then I am able to find the answers in me. Where they were all along."

DOCTOR ROBERT GRAHAM of the Graham Clan was a modernising influence in the Scottish/English border lands in the 1700s.

Quarries were dug because of him, mills established, new houses built, and rivers were tamed by safe and solid bridges.

At one of these bridges, some time ago, a memorial plaque said of him, "By the grace of God, he served his generation."

May we each, in our own way, do the same.

THE Lady Of The House laid flowers on a family grave, then chatted with a poorly dressed older woman who was doing the same.

They talked for a few moments, then the other woman nodded at her flowers.

"They're only plastic," she said. "I hope you don't think that means my love for him was as fake as they are."

My sweetheart paused.

"There's something they say about plastic. And usually it's a bad thing, but not in this instance."

"What's that," the other woman asked.

"That it lasts for ever."

*A*LTHOUGH *to summer we bid farewell,*
Bright days still lie ahead,
As our landscape is transformed
To gold and fiery red.
Silvery webs on hedgerows
Glisten in a frosty sun,
Kids scrunching through fallen leaves,
Autumn has begun.

Embrace the gifts of this glorious land,
From the magic of nature's hand.

Pamela Ramage

Autumn brings its own joys.

shutterstock

Saturday — October 15

HE sent us a regular cheque for a lot of years after hearing me talk about this good cause. I said perhaps he would like to come along and see first-hand where his money was going.

"I'm far too busy. That's why I need you," he replied.

We took his generous gifts, but I would have given them back if he would only have given something else.

What's that? I would have had him give himself the time to be kind in person – for the joy it might have brought him.

Sunday — October 16

IN his letter to the Philippians, St Paul encourages us to look to the good and noble in life and make them the subjects of our conversations, rather than the other nonsense.

I have no doubt Canadian poet Edna Jaques had that letter in mind when she wrote:

"If there be beauty in a world of ill,

A quiet valley where a church bell rings,

Where there is faith and love and little homes,

Speak on these things . . ."

Monday — October 17

IMAGINE you're in a boat on a lake. You lie back, close your eyes, feel the gentle rock of the boat and the breeze on your skin.

It's a completely peaceful and happy moment. Then someone jolts your boat. You sit up, angry at being disturbed, prepared to tell the other person off for their carelessness and for spoiling your day.

Then you see the boat is empty. It just happened to drift your way.

Then you realise your anger was all your own doing and, in this instance, was for nothing.

So many of the things that bump into us in real life are also "empty vessels", with as little purpose and point. But we still get angry.

If we must get angry at all, get angry at deliberate unkindness, and even then, only if it helps makes the situation better!

Tuesday — October 18

THE little group of walkers in raincoats and wellington boots consisted of two mothers and their six children.

Their attire was very appropriate. The day was starting to dull down, there was rain in the wind and muddy puddles galore.

"Are you having fun?" I asked a little one.

"We are going to have the best day ever. If we believe it will be, it will be!"

I had a glance around. Her mum was smiling; her mum's friend was smiling. I was smiling, too. She had made a very good start!

"I do believe you will," I said.

Wednesday — October 19

HARRY had been walking in the park with his granddaughter, Amy. The colours of the leaves caught both their attentions.

"It's funny, we rarely comment on the leaves when they are green and supposedly in their prime, but when they are almost done, they take our breath away," Harry remarked.

"Maybe leaves are like people," Amy replied. "We think they have a prime then a time of decline when, actually, they grow full and just get more magnificent!"

"I couldn't swear to it," Harry told me afterwards, "but I think there was a gentle squeezing of my hand as she spoke."

Thursday — October 20

SKIP is a good old age physically. If I were to age his spirit, I would not be able to pin it down.

I asked how he was recently.

"Playing at getting old," he said. "Learning new things every day."

I commented that his was an unusual attitude.

"I have spent many decades doing everything else," he replied. "Now it's time to learn about something new; something I have never experienced before. I've always liked learning new stuff."

What can I say?

HE doesn't just automatically make me happy every minute of every day," she said. "But I am committed to him and that means I get to see him in a lot of different 'weathers', and I get to look for the good in him, whether he's at his best or not.

"I usually find something there that is more than worth the effort it takes to look for it.

I will spare the blushes of the good wife who said this, and the hapless but lucky man she was talking about, but it occurred to me that was also an excellent way to live a life: commit to it and always keep looking for the best.

My sweetheart and I honestly believe you will find it if you do.

Saturday — October 22

KIRSTEN and her mother, Grace, were visiting a zoo that prides itself on its ecological efforts. It is working to restore the fortunes of several endangered species.

Looking at all the different signs, Grace wondered which species they should visit first.

Kirsten, with a mischievous glint in her eye, pointed one out saying it might be the most endangered of them all. The sign was on a door and it said *Gentlemen*.

Without missing a beat, Grace assured her daughter that gentlemen would be around for a while yet and they needn't go through that door.

I, for one, hope we don't disappoint her!

Sunday — October 23

THE Scottish village of Fintry had an unofficial slogan. "Out of the world and into Fintry."

As lovely as the village is, I am sure the slogan was referring to the peace, beauty and scenery – the things of God's world – that surrounded it. While "the world" was the industrial mess we made.

Instead of the occasional holiday in nature's tranquillity, wouldn't it be better if we brought more of God's world into ours?

Monday — October 24

THE charity shop was busy, so the big man might be excused for knocking a bag off a rail without noticing it.

A little woman noticed it. When she saw he wasn't turning back, she picked it up, put it on the rail and patted it, as if reassuring it that it was back where it belonged.

It is hardly worth mentioning, except for highlighting how grateful we should be to the people – and there are bound to be many in my case – who quietly take care of – and put right – the little disasters we unwittingly leave behind us.

Tuesday — October 25

IN the grounds of Alloway Auld Kirk lies William Burnes. His gravestone bears a tribute from his son, the poet Robert Burns.

Strangely, some might think, the son doesn't only focus on the father's virtues. In the last line, he adds, "Even his failings lean'd to virtue's side."

No-one's perfect. But if our shortcomings are a benefit to people, then we will have come as close to perfection as is allowed.

Wednesday — October 26

WE lost a much-loved pet recently, and this old story helped the tears flow.

A dog spirit waiting to go to earth was trying out his moves for God. He raised an ear and let his tongue hang out.

"Humans love that," God replied.

"What about this?" the dog asked, chasing his tail.

"That makes them laugh," God replied.

"And this?" The dog fetched a ball.

"That makes them happy, too," God replied.

"Do I do anything that makes them sad?" the dog asked.

God thought about it, but couldn't speak for the lump in his throat.

"What?" the dog asked.

"Never mind," God replied. "I'll tell you when you get back."

Thursday — October 27

A GATHERING of pre-school children were discussing – of all things – the weather! Perhaps they had heard their parents do the same often enough.

Then one girl, arguing with another over the nature of clouds, turned to her mother for adjudication.

"What are clouds for, Mum?"

Taken aback, the mother started to explain the evaporation cycle, and the importance of rain in giving flowers a drink.

The other girl interrupted her.

"My gran says they're to help us appreciate when the sun shines."

Silently promising to explain more later, the mother told her own daughter, "Her gran is right."

Friday — October 28

THERE are only so many paths in this country park," my companion said. "We have walked them several times – but I'm not bored!"

We talked about how the seasons, the weather, even the direction we took always showed us something different. We agreed we both loved that.

Further along the way, she stepped off the path and brushed some long grass aside to reveal a plaque on a rock. It read: *Nature, in all its diversity, grants us a glimpse into the heart of God, which is nothing but love!*

It seems someone else had the same idea.

Saturday — October 29

I HADN'T visited my childhood home since I left it, aged five. Years later, there I was, standing across the road from it.

It looked as I remembered it: the bay window, the step in the path, the back garden raised. But there was no connection. It struck me as just an ordinary house.

Then, on a whim, I knelt down and there it was! Home!

The world is a very different place when we look at it from a child's perspective.

Sunday — October 30

WE met at a family party. It was noisy, so talking was difficult. But when a mutual friend pointed her out, I just had to tell her how big an influence her husband had been on me.

I was warned she had dementia and might not understand, but I had to try!

On my third attempt at trying to make myself heard, she understood what I was saying and her face lit up.

"Oh, wonderful!" she cried. "I'll be sure to tell him you said that when I see him."

Having nothing more to say, I thanked her and left, confused. For a moment I thought that she had forgotten her husband had died years ago. If that were the case, then I was glad I had at least made her happy.

But a look and a smile she sent my way later in the evening helped me understand.

It wasn't that her memory was weak, it was that her faith was strong enough to assure her that she would be able to pass my message on – in heaven.

Monday — October 31

A FRIEND posted on social media that all her electrics had blown and the only power she had was her mobile phone battery.

Jim's no electrician, but because his friend lives on her own and has mental health issues, he decided to make the drive.

Perhaps, if nothing else, he could buy fish and chips to keep her warm and fed.

At worst, she could complain to him.

Once he got there, he found an easy fix that would get her lights on until an electrician arrived.

Then he went for chips and they ate them together.

"I didn't know how I was going to help," Jim admitted to me. "But if I had never set out, the opportunity would never have found me."

Whenever you can, put yourself in the position for opportunity to find you and put you to good use.

November

Tuesday — November 1

IN his poem "A Winter Piece", William Cullen Bryant professes his love for all the seasons, but when November's winds blow he misses the herbs of the fields and the shade of the trees on sunnier days.

Missing them, he doesn't dismiss them. He thinks of them as old companions in a time of adversity. They have gone away for a while. He is glad to have known them and is sure they will return. Then he turns his attention to the different beauties that have arrived.

Miss what has gone, but appreciate what has arrived!

Wednesday — November 2

THE sloping stone steps led to the riverside. It had been raining for two days. Rivulets gathered from every direction and gutters overflowed. For that day, the steps became a waterfall.

"Wow!" I exclaimed, looking for the best angle to take a photo.

"Ridiculous," the man behind me said. "The council ought to clear the drains. Those folk with clogged-up gutters ought to be fined!"

It was the same scene and two different responses. A dramatic, unexpected waterfall, or a chance to complain? We choose how we see the world. We might at least choose a way that makes us happy – even when it's raining!

Thursday — November 3

ANDY has been searching for a girlfriend. Talking about his lack of success so far and his high hopes for the future, he said, "When I find Miss Right, I hope she makes me as miserable as the Lady Of The House makes you."

I was taken aback and opened my mouth to protest, but before I could speak he grinned and added, "When she's away!"

Well, OK, then!

Left to the elements.

Shutterstock.

Blairgowrie, Scotland.

Friday — November 4

I SAW a boy with a crocheted woollen blanket. One of those square ones with holes for children to stick their fingers through.

It took me back to sitting on a stool in front of a coal fire, with my grandmother to one side, crocheting those blankets from whatever wool she could find.

They were always for other people, to keep them or their children warm in the winter.

"But," she would say, "they keep my own knees cosy while I work on them."

Perhaps that's where I learned that, in helping others, we can't help but help ourselves.

Saturday — November 5

I WAS paying for shopping and the chat turned to families and how the checkout operator hadn't talked to her brother in eight years.

The next time I saw her, she announced, "I phoned him! We had a long chat and we're meeting for coffee next week."

She thinks I'm wonderful now! But I couldn't imagine anything I'd said having made such a difference.

Then I understood. I was the impartial stranger who listened and let her talk herself into doing something she'd wanted to do for eight years.

Sunday — November 6

THE faded sheet on the noticeboard was a reworking of the Ten Commandments by Basil Martin. I wondered if the writer was Reverend Basil Martin, pacifist and fighter for social justice in the late 1800s and early 1900s.

The "commandment" that caught my attention was, "Remember the weekday, to keep it holy, and the Sabbath will take care of itself!"

Either he thought six days of holiness would be habit-forming and the seventh would follow automatically, or that so much holiness would be such hard work that one day of rest would be in order.

Monday — November 7

"ALL you can do is your best." We hear that all the time, and doing your best is certainly a fine thing.

Let me add to that a possibly apocryphal, but certainly thought-provoking, story of Catherine Booth.

The granddaughter of the founder of the Salvation Army, William Booth, once told him she had done her best. She was surprised he told her she should have done better!

Seeing her distress, the General softened his tone, saying something like, "Of course, your best is all you can do. But you and God together can do better than that. Better than any of our bests."

Tuesday — November 8

THE two men were in deep conversation. They walked side by side, heads down, with hands clasped behind their backs. I noticed they even walked in step.

But they weren't the only ones "mirroring".

Behind one of them walked a boy of about four. He had his head down, his hands were clasped behind his back and every now and then he would skip to try to keep his little legs in time with theirs.

We teach our children more than we understand – and they learn less from what we say than from how we live.

Wednesday — November 9

THE Scottish preacher and writer George MacDonald might have been referring to November weather when, in his novel, "Adela Cathcart", he said: "But the night and the frost wake the sunshine of a higher world in our hearts."

It's nice to know the frost and night are good for something, isn't it?

But, you will notice, he didn't say it created the sunshine. He talks about it being awakened. It is already there!

At this time of year, we certainly need a little internal sunshine.

Find something that awakens yours!

JANE, our local choir mistress, is a wonderful lady, but she can be quite blunt at times. The rehearsals weren't going well. She had tried different approaches, then it all got too much.

"No!" she shouted. "You are singing like a bunch of amateurs!"

I imagined a mass walk-out. But no!

"Do you know what the word amateur means? It comes from the Latin 'amator', which means someone who does what they do for the love of it." She softened her tone until it was almost a plea. "So sing like you love it!"

And they did!

Friday — November 11

WE are not short of war memorials in this country, which is a sad yet beautiful thing.

My favourite memorial might be called graffiti. It is a name and a date scratched into one of the pillars in Winchester Cathedral, perhaps by someone listening to a sermon. It says, *Albert Gannon – 1944*, and a shield is scratched around it.

For me, Albert symbolises those who never made it home, were never mentioned on any memorial, but were loved all the same.

Lest we forget.

Saturday — November 12

DOCTOR ROBERT PROVINE died in 2019. Every article that mentions his death described him in the same way.

I read once that he said we laugh on average 30 times more when we are with friends than when we aren't. Apparently, Doctor Provine believed we wouldn't be laughing at jokes so much as laughing to show our friends how happy we were to have them there.

Which is a beautiful thought in itself. But it was overshadowed, when I looked him up, by the ubiquitous assertion that Doctor Provine was an "expert on laughter".

What a wonderful thing to be!

Sunday — November 13

THERE'S a story of a monk who confessed to his abbot, "I have fallen from grace. What should I do?"

He expected words of wisdom or condemnation. But the abbot replied, "You should get back up again."

A year later he returned with a similar confession. The abbot again told him, "You should get back up again."

That's the thing about grace: if you want to return, it will always be waiting for you.

Monday — November 14

THERE was a long queue at this particular counter. The shop assistant noticed an older man leave his place near the head of the queue and rejoin it at the end.

Each time he came close to being served, she saw him do the same thing. Then he left. The last man to speak to him explained.

"He wasn't shopping. He was just lonely. He thought a queue would be a good place to find nice people to chat to because we were all in the same situation."

When she told me this it made me think two things. The first was, how awful that anyone should be so lonely. The second was to be more sociable the next time I find myself in a queue. Just in case!

Tuesday — November 15

THERE'S joy in life, of course, like shards of sunlight in the sky,
But also clouds of troubles causing us a weary sigh.
They drain our spirits, weigh us down, they burden us with grief;
We try to cast them off but find, alas, there's no relief.
"I've not the strength to carry on," our tired spirits sigh,
Forgetting that we have a friend, who hears us when we cry.
He's one who never leaves us, he created us from dust,
He formed us in his image, ever worthy of our trust.
Remember him amidst despair and when your frail heart quails;
For there's beauty in the morning and a love which never fails.

Ewan Smith

I CONFESSED, a little shamefaced, that I hadn't done it after all.

"I was going to," I said. "I had the perfect opportunity, but I doubted myself too much."

"Do you do that often?" she asked. "Get stopped by your doubts?"

"It happens," I said, unwilling to commit to how often.

"Do you ever doubt your doubts?" she asked. "Do you ever let doubts about your doubts stop you doubting?"

"I . . . well . . ."

Now that I think about it, it does seem only fair.

I PUT a tip on the counter. The waitress said, "That's too much! Please take it back!"

"It's deserved. You take such good care of all of us," I replied.

"That's because you're my favourites," she admitted.

I wasn't conceited enough to think she meant me. I also didn't believe she was flattering or deceiving.

I think she has discovered the secret of believing everyone who comes into the café is deserving of being treated like a favourite.

I wondered how far that stretched into her personal life. Pretty far, I imagined.

I left the tip. And my admiration.

HAVE you ever gone along with something you shouldn't because a family member wanted it?

There's a comfort in doing what your "tribe" do, a feeling of belonging, but it can lead us astray.

In his essay "Self Reliance", Ralph Waldo Emerson addresses the notion that "blood is thicker than water", but adds, "All men have my blood and I have all men's", so if he was to do a thing it ought to be something that is for the benefit of all.

How big is your family?

I FOUND myself standing behind a playgroup the other day.

Waiting for the lights to change on a busy road, the leaders asked specific older children to take the hands of the littler ones.

A cute moment, but nothing much to speak of – until I noticed how disappointed some of the older children were at not getting to hold a hand.

"There are only a few needing looked after and we're trying to make sure everyone gets a turn," one of the leaders explained.

Those playgroup leaders had somehow created an environment where it was seen as a treat to get to help others.

Now, if only society's leaders could do the same thing.

Sunday — November 20

T HE minister was telling the Sunday school about patron saints: who they were and why they were revered, the great deeds they had done and how they were supposed to look after particular countries from on high.

Knowing he had children whose families were from Wales, Ireland, England and Scotland in the group, he asked, "Who is your patron saint?"

Six-year-old Caroline raised her hand and proudly announced, "My grampa!"

Now, I know Caroline's grampa. And except for the fact that he is still with us and has never slayed a dragon, I can't say she was wrong!

Monday — November 21

H ARRY had been in with a group of old friends. After discussing all the things you aren't supposed to – politics, religion and whatever – someone proposed the notion that in any election the moral authority always lay with the losing side, while the majority were usually in the wrong.

"The debate went on and on," Harry told me. "In fact, it started to get quite heated, so we decided to settle it with a vote.

"The side who were for it won by a stonking majority!

Tuesday — November 22

I **AM** going to agitate some fellow book-lovers now. I dog-ear pages. I sympathise with the notion that it is a form of vandalism.

But whenever I make such a mark, or see such a mark made from before, I know there is something extraordinary on that page. Something worth remembering or sharing.

It's the same with people. Those marked in some way by life usually have the best stories within them.

Damage is never to be welcomed, but if it comes with a good story to tell then it might, on occasion, be excused.

Wednesday — November 23

I **WAS** looking for a translation of a line of Hebrew. So I copied and pasted it into a search engine on my laptop.

Once the search box recognised the language, it reversed itself to accommodate the fact that Hebrew reads from right to left.

I've had this laptop a few years and had no idea it, or the search engine, could do that. It occurred to me that I had only the faintest idea of its capabilities.

I mentioned this to the Lady Of The House.

"Yet every person you ever met," she replied, "was at least a hundred times more complex. And you think you understood them."

Now that gave me serious pause for thought!

Thursday — November 24

I **N** 1928, novelist and schoolmaster Ernest Raymond compiled a book of his favourite passages from literature, offering his thoughts. At one point he comments on the tendency for cynicism among the literary greats of his time.

"But if despair is the truth for the majority," he wrote, "it is no truth for me. Something instinctive and elemental rises up in me to resist such doctrines. I believe that indignant force to be life itself, rising to prove itself more good than bad!"

It's a decision we have always made for ourselves. Personally, I agree with Mr Raymond – and life!

Sometimes nature's "damage" makes a beautiful scene.

Shutterstock.

Bishopthorpe near York, England.

Friday — November 25

COLOURS blaze and then they fade:
The year is growing old.
Trees stand bare in misty air,
Yet winter's still on hold.
It's in this quiet interlude
Our thoughts we can collect,
As we look forward and look back
To plan and to reflect.

John Darley

Saturday — November 26

GERMANY is a beautiful country. I like to visit, but my language skills have never exceeded what I learned in school.

I was telling Mary how much I'd like to learn a second language.

"One day," I added.

"Right words, wrong order," she said. "Turn 'one day' into 'day one' and you go from something never getting done to this being the first day of making it happen."

All right, then. Day One – or *Tag Eins*.

Sunday — November 27

ROBERT LOUIS STEVENSON was not a notably religious man. Asked by a priest if he was a Christian, he denied the charge. But there is no doubt that he was a spiritual man.

Travelling through France on a donkey, he spent a night sleeping under the stars on a wooded hillside. Waking, he had a strong feeling that he had been gifted something special. After loading his packs and walking off, he dropped coins on the grass to the amount of a night's lodgings, hoping some poor person would find them.

Whether it was God or nature he was thanking did not concern him. He simply felt he ought to give thanks.

It's a deep part of us, this need to give thanks, whether it be by prayer, by good deeds or by loving one another. I know it myself.

I never imagine the one the great novelist and poet felt he was paying saying, "You owe me." It's always, "You're welcome!"

Monday — November 28

I **HAVE** a book from 1929 called "Joy's Loom" by Wilhelmina Stitch. It's full of beautiful little vignettes, but nowhere does it explain the title. One thought might be that "joy" is something woven on the loom of life; it's a lot of "threads" coming together – and it takes a fair bit of work, as any loom operator will tell you.

That might be as good a definition of joy as I have ever heard. A lot of things have to come together and a lot of work has to go into it to make the pleasure seem spontaneous and effortless.

Would joy be such a delight if we didn't know at least some of the effort that had gone into bringing it about?

Tuesday — November 29

I **T** was an impulse buy in a charity shop. "Selected English Essays", edited by George Loane. It had been issued to a girl called Rita.

The essays were intended to stretch the mind. Throughout, there were sections underlined and questions pencilled in the margins.

Pasted to the inside covers and inserted between pages were newspaper cuttings recording the adventures of the Renfrewshire Ladies football club.

Certain names were ticked, like our student knew them. I wonder if she played. If she did, I would guess that young Rita had the same ambition as many ancient Greeks – *Mens sana in corpore sano*.

In other words, a healthy mind in a healthy body!

Wednesday — November 30

T **HE** book "The Specialist" tells the story of Lem Putt, who decided to specialise in building privies in a time before indoor plumbing. He was soon very much in demand. Those who needed an outdoor toilet called for Lem.

At the end of any stressful day, he'd drive his truck to a hill with a view of his favourite privy and rest in the knowledge that it could not have been built any better.

There's a lot of comfort in knowing a thing has been done properly – and has been done properly by you! So, assuming no-one needs a privy near you, what would your specialism be?

Anything can be fascinating if we maintain our childlike curiosity.

Shutterstock.

December

Thursday — December 1

IT wasn't a day for going out, so I turned on the radio while I waited for the kettle to boil. They were talking about aluminium. Blah!

The kettle boiled and I should have switched the radio off, but someone said something interesting. Then someone else replied with a fact I hadn't heard before.

Pretty soon I was engrossed and I drank my tea listening to the rest of the programme.

How had that happened? Well, I was listening to experts in the field, and their passion, knowledge and enthusiasm captured my attention. It would be the same with anything. If you listen to experts on any subject, you find the subject isn't as boring as you thought.

I'd go as far as to say there isn't one single part of this world, this creation, that isn't fascinating, if we only look closely enough.

So I put my shoes on and went looking!

Friday — December 2

I KNOW a lot of poets. Wonderful people they are. Very few of them make any money at all from their poetry. That's not why they do it.

I was thinking about this after Amy, who lives in North Carolina, told me about her ninety-three-year-old dad. They'd been recalling how he used to sing her to sleep when she was little.

Apparently, he sang her poems by Robert Louis Stevenson put to music. One was about the wind and one was about the foreign lands a child might see when climbing up a tree. Even today she can recite them.

Stevenson actually did make money as a poet, but I think anyone with a poetic heart might swap a great many royalties for the notion that, one day in the far future, someone might sing their daughter to sleep using their words. Don't you?

IT'S December. When do you put your tree up?

The Ghost of Christmas Past in Charles Dickens's "A Christmas Carol" is a variable, changing figure, but for Scrooge he seems most like a human candle. His head glows with a bright, warm light, but under his arm he carries a large metal candle-snuffer which others – including Scrooge – have apparently made for him.

Scrooge does, at one point, try to make him wear it. The light dims, but doesn't go out.

Some of us might behave like Scrooges when it comes to the right time to put up trees, but it doesn't really matter. What matters is that our "Bah humbugs" should always be in jest. No good can come from dimming the light of someone else's Christmas.

Instead, get into the spirit (of Christmases past and present), whenever it arrives. Be a festive candle yourself. Add to the light!

Sunday — December 4

IN an old episode of "Doctor Who", the Doctor plays chess for the future of the universe.

At one point his opponent asks him to sacrifice his most valuable piece for the life of a child. He doesn't hesitate to topple his queen and seems to have lost. But the child knew something the Doctor didn't, enabling him to save the universe.

It's a writing technique, crafted and placed to maximum effect. You will find it in many books, films and TV shows. It works because it gives a sense of good overcoming in the end. For me, though, it speaks of something deeper.

We are not the masters of the game; it is not ours to win. The game is God's. He decides the outcome. Until then, we take care of one another.

Depending on your take on faith, we are either an expression of the Divine or his children. If we sacrifice an innocent in a war, or a person sleeping rough, or a neighbour who does things we don't like, we sacrifice the creator of the game. In winning at any cost, we automatically lose.

We understand this when we see it on a screen or a page.

May we understand it in our own lives.

SAINT FRANCIS OF ASSISI is famous for – amongst other things – talking to the animals. My neighbour does something similar.

I often hear him say, "Morning, Ted!", "How are you, Harry?" and "Hey, Blue!"

Ted is a little Yorkshire terrier who barks at him the whole time. Henry is a cat who sits atop a fence post and watches him pass by in silence. Blue (or Big Blue) is what his granddaughter named his car.

I might be tempted to laugh. But I would also love to be on first-name terms with the world every morning as he is.

Tuesday — December 6

INTRODUCING the Lady Of The House to the film "Truly, Madly, Deeply", I felt I should explain. Even though it's a sublime love story, it's not without bleaker parts, dealing with grief and loss as it does.

I once watched "It's A Wonderful Life" with a friend, having sung its praises. The video player chewed the tape at George Bailey's darkest moment, before things were made right again. Now he's convinced it's the most depressing film ever.

"But that's life," the Lady Of The House told me. "The possibility of happy endings is what gets us through the difficult times. And the more difficult those times are, they sweeter the happy endings are.

"You really need both!"

Wednesday — December 7

THE bark had been stripped from the side of the tree years ago. An artistic soul saw the bare wood and painted planks there: a little arched window, a letter-box, with a pint of milk at the bottom. They even fixed a real doorknob to it, completing the look of an elfin door.

Harry, normally the most sensible of fellows, looked at it.

"Is it strange," he asked, "that I have a strong urge to turn it and see if the door opens?"

Not wise, maybe, but no, not strange. Wonder knows no age.

The company of friends can bring such joy at Christmas.

Shutterstock.

*A*S most of us are fortunate
As Christmastime draws near,
To know that we'll be safe and warm
And filled with Christmas cheer,
We really need to think of those
Who're lonely, sick or old,
Or those who'll spend their Christmas
In a doorway in the cold.
We're lucky, and it's up to us
To give a helping hand,
However small, to try to spread
God's love throughout the land.

Eileen Hay

A **CERTAIN** foolish man discovered that his neighbours' income had taken a hit recently, so he tried to give them some money as a gift.

The mother of the family insisted that they didn't need it and politely refused.

The foolish man believed that he knew better and persisted – to the point of becoming a nuisance.

The mother explained that their basic bills were covered and, beyond that, their needs were simple and easily met.

She told him that she and her husband and their two boys had been to the beach (on a day when he would never have ventured out of the house), how they had yelled at the wind, jumped over inlets, and how her son had claimed a sandbar as a sovereign nation.

She told of all the fun they had had chasing each other with seaweed.

He knew this wasn't an unusual day for them.

So the foolish man laid the money aside for a time it might actually be useful.

Then he readjusted his ideas of what being wealthy really meant.

Saturday — December 10

IT had all the makings of a perfect rainbow, but it didn't quite complete the arc. It rose up out of the sea and dropped towards the golf course, but never seemed to arrive.

You see, offshore a thunderstorm was brewing. The pillar of colour almost seemed on fire against the bank of black cloud.

Over the clubhouse the sky was still a bright clear blue, and the colours faded into it until they couldn't be seen.

If our times of adversity do one good thing, they make our blessings stand out all the brighter.

Sunday — December 11

IMAGINE you told some random stranger you loved them. You might reasonably expect them to say, "But you don't even know me!"

Now, think of all the people in the world who hate others for no good reason. Somehow that is accepted as something that just is.

If it's OK to hate for no good reason, then, in a fair world, it must be OK to love for no good reason.

What's that you say? "It's not a fair world?"

If it's OK to assume that, why isn't it OK for me to assume it is?

All that's left to do is love unreasonably. As Jesus would have it!

Monday — December 12

DECEMBER weather. It doesn't have much to recommend it, am I right?

Thomas de Quincey, the 19th-century essayist, would argue that I was wrong. In 1821, he wrote, "Surely everybody is aware of the divine pleasures which attend a wintry fireside, candles at four o'clock, warm hearth-rugs, tea, a fair tea-maker, shutters closed, curtains flowing in ample draperies on the floor, whilst the wind and rain are raging audibly without."

You haven't tried those things yet? Or their modern equivalents? Why, December weather would be positively unpleasant without them!

CAROLINE bought a rock tumbler. A regular beach walker, she finds lots of stones that might benefit from a polish.

The tumbler is a small motorised drum. Water, grit and stones are put inside, then it is switched on. A week or so of constant tumbling through water and grit smooths the rough edges and gives the stones a polished look. A few weeks more and the stones might be almost gem-like.

It reminded me of a saying of debatable origin but authentic wisdom: "Let your failures refine you, not define you."

Tumble, but rise up again – more polished for the experience!

ERIC LIDDELL became famous as the Olympic athlete who refused to run in the heats for his best racing distance because they were being held on a Sunday.

Instead, he ran in a race where he wasn't favoured – and set a new Olympic record!

I asked his daughter, Patricia Russell, what she thought would have happened had he run.

"He would have lost." She didn't hesitate. "He would have broken something important to him."

What must it be like to have something so important to you that you sacrifice worldly success for it; something that lifts you higher and makes you run faster having kept it?

WORRIED about buying the right Christmas gift? Afraid your finances might not be up to the job? The 19th-century English essayist Leigh Hunt offered up this advice.

"A poor man, if he is generous and understood to be so, may make the very poorest of presents and give it an exquisite value, for his heart and his understanding will accompany it."

Being known to be generous is a good thing. Gifts given with your heart and understanding behind them will always be well received.

ALFRED, **LORD TENNYSON**, was writing about taverns and strong drink when he wrote, "I look at all things as they are. But through a kind of glory."

Good for him. And I hope his head wasn't too sore in the morning.

There is another way, though, of seeing that glory.

Look at all things as they are. See how they fit with the world around them. Think of the purposes they serve. Ask how they came to be and wonder at the glorious design of it all.

Saturday — December 17

LEGEND has it that Richard Bernhard Smith wrote the Christmas song "Winter Wonderland" while being treated for tuberculosis. His fiancé would visit as often as she could and they would go for walks in the snow-covered woods around the hospital.

Neither the trees nor the snow made it a wonderland. Rather, the presence of love worked that magic.

It's a beautiful song, and deserves to be remembered.

Smith died of TB shortly afterwards, but he left us more than just a lovely song; he left us the lesson that beauty can still be made in the midst of hard times.

Sunday — December 18

HE was in the grip of addiction, but he also felt called to God. When he told me he had enrolled in a theology course, I bought him the main textbook.

When it arrived, I asked the Lady Of The House if she had a bag I could wrap it in.

She picked one that had wrapped a gift of Turkish delight from a friend's holiday. It advertised two Turkish shops: the Eternity Gold and Diamonds shop and the Faith Gift Shop. Two words were printed much larger than the others. So when I gave him his theology text book, the two words he saw first were "Eternity" and "Faith".

It was only afterwards that I wondered if that had been planned. Either by God – or my household angel.

Beauty can always be found, even in the hardest of times.

Mellonlahti nature trail, Finland.

IT is less than a week to Christmas. The children will undoubtedly be excited. At least, I sincerely hope they are. And that excitement is usually a joy to behold.

I thought I'd share the opinion of 19th-century English poet Francis Thompson on the nature of children.

"Know you what it is to be a child?" he asked. "It is to be something very different to the man of today . . . it is to believe in love, to believe in loveliness, to believe in belief, it is to be so little that the elves can reach to whisper in your ear."

Can there be anything to compare with that way of being?

We might not now be the children we once were, and, try as we might, we can never regain that condition, but the next best thing to being like that is surely to be protecting, appreciating and loving that.

In doing so, we may find ourselves remembering how to believe in belief.

Tuesday — December 20

THERE is a local authority children's home near us. It's a short-stay facility for children between the ages of nine and sixteen.

Each year at this time I visit with tubs of chocolates.

For security's sake, while I know how many rooms the place has, I am never told how many residents there are. I never see any of the children and I never get past the front door.

It seems like a different staff member answers the door each time I arrive, and I have to explain who I am and what I am doing – which is as it should be.

This year, I was explaining myself to someone when another staff member saw me from a distance.

She must have remembered me, because she shouted over, "It's OK, Sheena, he's – what was it you said last year? – he's a neighbour!"

And suddenly the situation was fine; the gifts were handed over.

I walked away thinking, "God bless the staff. God bless the children. And what an honoured title 'neighbour' is."

H EY," I grunted.
"How are you?" He seemed genuinely interested.

"Wet!" The rain was drumming off my cap and seeping through the shoulders of my jacket.

"It could be worse," he said. "Some folk pray for this weather."

I said no more. It was OK for him: I could barely see his face for all the protective gear he had on. He wasn't going to get wet.

He took the covering off a hole by the side of the path, spread a waterproof sheet beside the hole and lay down on it.

He lowered the upper half of his body into the hole, then, with bulky gloves, goggles and a hard hat fastened under his chin, he went to work, upside-down, on some newly laid electrical cables in what was basically a puddle surrounded by mud.

I headed home for breakfast and dry clothes. This was the start of the working day for him.

It could be worse, I told myself. I tried imagining that the rain was a welcome shower of life-giving water, as some would have found it.

I succeeded – a little. But it was enough, along with my encounter with the electricity man, to remind me that, to whatever degree we can, we make our days, not the weather.

F ROM yards away, the tree looked asleep for the winter.
Which is how it should have been, after all. It was December and we'd just been given a snow warning by the Met Office.

As I got closer, though, I saw blossoms. They were small, but there were lots of them, with white petals and orangey-yellow stamens. A delight on an unspring-like morning!

A wiser man might have known what sort of tree it was and explained that this was normal. I could only think that I had judged it harshly by my own expectations. Here it was, being quietly beautiful against all the odds.

I fear I sometimes do the same with people. Before I judge anyone by my expectations of them, may I get close enough to see who they really are.

Friday — December 23

YOU know those flowers and cacti that bloom around Christmastime? Is it just the natural world singing its praise? I wouldn't be surprised at all.

I'm sure a biologist could give us a fine explanation as to why some plants will blossom only in the darkest times. And it would be fascinating, I am sure.

But for now I will content myself with knowing this one thing: that there are people who do the same!

Saturday — December 24

CAR tyres present a particular problem for recyclers. Made to be indestructible, there are mountains of them just waiting for someone to come up with another use for them.

The primary school near us bought seven or eight different-sized lorry tyres and piled them in an inverted cone in the playground. They painted them, decorated them, hung light over them – and there it was. Their own, imaginative, beautiful and indestructible Christmas tree.

What an ingeniously creative idea, taking something from the refuse and giving a previously unthought-of purpose.

It occurred to me that one of the children in that school might just invent a way of properly recycling tyres, or something equally as impressive.

The coming generation will surely make its own mistakes, but I believe they will solve many of the problems our generations caused and make the world a better place.

My faith is in the future. My faith is in children.

The child whose birth we are waiting to celebrate was a baby like no other. He was (and is) a gift to the whole world and a saviour for us all.

But the children who wait in breathless anticipation for Christmas morning have this in common with him – they, too, are gifts to the world, each one of them full of immense possibility.

Nurture them and, in a very earthly way, they might just save us all. Nurture Jesus in our hearts and he will save us in every other way.

My faith in both of those things is indestructible.

PEOPLE debate the authenticity of celebrating Jesus's birth in winter. Jeff, who is a pastor now, doesn't mind.

"So many things had gone wrong," he explained. "It was like the winter of my soul. But when I had nothing else, I found Jesus was there.

"He always had been there, of course, but the depths of our personal winter is when we see him shine all the clearer.

"Whether he was born in winter or in spring, it doesn't matter. He is the Lord of our winters and the promise of better things to come."

Monday — December 26

IN a vain attempt at working off some Christmas calories, the Lady Of The House and I took a walk along the shore front.

The sky and the sea were grey and empty, as befitting the day after the celebrations when next to nothing gets done.

But they were also full of potential: a blank canvas for any kind of weather to be painted on.

A splash of colour caught my eye. Then another. Then another.

Of course, we decided to investigate.

Someone had decorated a whole row of benches with strands of tinsel.

They had bought cards from Save The Children, written uplifting messages on them and attached them to the benches.

One said: *You might not think your family are much, but they are the jewels of your life. Treasure them.*

Another said: *Check on your neighbours and people you haven't seen for a while. It won't do any harm and it might do a lot of good.*

A third said: *There is no getting away from it – this year has been tough, but next year hasn't been written yet. So lift your head, raise your eyes and aim for bigger and better!*

They are random thoughts, but good ones, offered from the anonymous decorators to the world.

And from my sweetheart and I to you: God bless!

Tuesday — December 27

IN his story "The Grand Inquisitor", Russian novelist Fyodor Dostoevsky wrote, "To love a person means to see them as God intended them."

Too far-fetched? Well, they say God came down to earth once as the baby boy who grew to be Jesus Christ. For 30 years, no-one noticed anything unusual about him!

Perhaps we don't need to be so different to be loved. Perhaps we needn't always strive for some impossible standard, or feel like failures. Perhaps we just need to be seen through eyes that understand what – and how wonderful – we can be.

Wednesday — December 28

I HELPED Thomas from his chair to the piano stool. Aged ninety-something, he was quite frail. He looked at the keys for a few seconds and I wondered if he had the strength to play.

But he proceeded to play "Moonlight Sonata" all the way through for us.

"The sound coming out of that piano was glorious!" I told him loudly, because he doesn't hear so well.

"Good, good," he replied. "It was glorious in my soul and in my memory as well. It's just the bit in between . . ." he held up his hands ". . . that gets a bit worn."

If only we could hear the music of each other's souls instead of only looking at the worn exteriors they are dressed in.

Thursday — December 29

I REMEMBER as a child waking up to frost on the inside of a metal-framed, single-paned bedroom window and inspecting its bright and delicate patterns up close.

As winter tightened its grip on the world, even the frost came in from the cold. We children added our variations to the designs Jack Frost left across the inside of the glass, with small, pink and increasingly numb fingertips.

We might think that a shame these days. But somehow I remember it as a wonder!

THE thrill of Christmas eases
As the year draws to its close,
Allowing for reflection,
To remember things, and those
Who shared the journey with us,
Making time a pleasure spent,
Their love and warmth and friendship
Life's finest testament.
We'll take such treasured memories
Into the coming year,
And even in uncertainty,
They'll never disappear.
There may be paths unknown to us
Which we will have to take,
But always there beside us,
Making clear what seems opaque,
Is God our father, whom we trust
To guide us safely through
Those days and weeks which, when they're shared,
Give life a broader view.

John Darley

I'VE always been curious about why the Scots call New Year's Eve Hogmanay.

The best explanation I have ever heard came from someone for whom English is a second language, and was a mistake!

Before they travelled to the big celebrations in Edinburgh, Caroline told a foreign friend it was a Hogmanay party. He repeated the unfamiliar name to her a few times before settling on, "Hug many?"

She was about to tell him that was wrong, when she realised it should be right.

There have been times recently when hugging was not advised. We all felt the loss. But – if it's safe – I can't think of a better way to end one year and begin a new one.

Hug many, my friends. While staying safe, hug as many as you can!

Shutterstock.

Happy New Year!

"Friendship is the golden thread that ties the heart of all the world"

John Evelyn

PEFC Certified

This product is from sustainably managed forests and controlled sources

PEFC/46-31-13   www.pefc.ro